echoes from the borderlands

study one: call you when I get home

Valeria Luiselli   Ricardo Giraldo   Leo Heiblum

INTRODUCTION

Kamilah N. Foreman and Humberto Moro

Echoes from the Borderlands is a collective formed by Valeria Luiselli, Ricardo Giraldo, and Leo Heiblum, and the title of a twenty-four-hour sound piece in the making about the histories of violence across the U.S.–Mexico border. Its duration is not a reflection of the Earth's daily rotation but rather the time it takes to drive the length of the border from the Pacific Ocean to the Gulf of Mexico, a voyage through terrain contested socially, politically, and economically, yet where life somehow prevails.

The subject matter is grounded in the specificities of the border since the Gadsden Purchase of 1853–54, a nineteenth-century sale of land from Mexico to the U.S. that solidified the boundary as it is recognized today. Previously, these lands had been fought over by Native nations, the Spanish crown, and the Mexican and U.S. governments, and since then have been areas of intrastate violence owing to the interventions of individual citizens, local law enforcement, and militias. The more famous instances of malice and brutality—gunfights and lynchings, among others—are re-performed through reenactments in sites like Tombstone, Arizona, within a full-fledged tourism economy that presents white violence performed by white actors against Indigenous, brown, and black peoples, historical erasures with inherently racial and gendered dimensions.[1]

Throughout this piece, one can dive deeply into the material history of the border while also learning about reservations and detention centers; eugenics; and the extractive economies of mining, oil, and water. As this chapbook's map indicates, the borderlands are more than the legal line made visible by fences, checkpoints, and rivers. The artists have traveled up to one hundred miles from the border to research, document, and present ways of being that are under constant negotiation precisely because of their proximity to the demarcation.

The sonic base of the work is what the artists have designated the "canvas," a layer of binaural and quadraphonic recordings taken during their journeys. Even when nearly silent, the canvas is ever present. On top of it, they have woven archival materials, their interviews with residents and contemporary thinkers, and other voices—authored by Luiselli—who provide poignant commentary along the way. In addition, the artists have created various recurring sonic motifs, such as a modified recording of the wind against a saguaro cactus thorn, which provide aesthetic and potentially emotional cues to the listener.

A series of "echoes" or, to use the artists' term, a "sonic essay"—where does it all begin? An echo is sonic energy as it bounces back from a reflective surface and can seem to distort, contrast, or augment the initial referent. For the visually inclined, echoes are like mirrors, but ones modified by distance and a delay in time, rather than light. Echoes imply movement and a non-static understanding of the past. Furthermore, as Luiselli writes in her novel *Lost Children Archive* (2019), “A camera can capture an entire portion of a landscape in a single impression; but a microphone, even a parabolic one, can sample only fragments and details.”[2] The recordings that compose *Echoes* are fundamentally samplings, fragments of fragments, edited by the artists and joined with their imaginative responses, verbal or sonic, in an exchange of nonfiction and fiction. The work operates as a set of counternarratives that resuscitate Indigenous, brown, and black perspectives, especially those of women, largely ignored in conventional histories.

Echoes thus offers a means of repair. The work’s incisive connections between seemingly contradictory or disparate parts of the American story, such as fertile lands and forced sterilization, belie the ease with which one engages the piece. We simply listen. However, through “hearing and recording those stories over and over again,” we become active agents in this recovery “so that they come back, always, to haunt and shame us” in what might be the only means to “grant any justice.”[3] Despite the intense subject matter, the piece includes ideas of hope, in part via the implied futurity of youth. The sounds of kids at play or a child’s understanding of the Earth—“a wet round rock”—also attest to how much history is ongoing activity, created in the moment and later inscribed by everyday people.[4] Beyond the present, *Echoes from the Borderlands* suggests new ways for how history can be energized, rewritten, and deployed.

This expansiveness is amplified by the artists’ choice of medium. By using sound, which is inherently ephemeral, they transcend limits of time and space. With recorded media, sound is nomadic as well: Visitors to Dia’s galleries in winter 2024–25 can experience *Echoes* with others, collectively, while it is also accessible online from nearly anywhere across the globe.

Dia’s support for *Echoes* fits within our legacy of championing Land art in the American West, from Walter De Maria’s *The Lightning Field* (1977) in New Mexico to Robert Smithson’s *Spiral Jetty* (1970) and Nancy Holt’s *Sun Tunnels* (1973–76) in Utah. These works variously incorporate the landscape and speak to humanity’s symbiotic and at times oppositional relationship to the Earth and cosmos. With the presentation of *Echoes*, Dia proffers other perspectives, particularly those of the peoples most affected by colonial and environmental violence and their ongoing manifestations. This project is also in keeping with our newest site, Cameron Rowland’s *Depreciation* (2018), whose astonishing conceit moves land completely out of the totalizing context of capitalism, through a restrictive covenant and a long-term loan to Dia that evacuate it of all financial worth. Yet, in both projects, the land is not an abstraction.

It exists within other relational schema beyond conventional values or the legacies of slavery and Manifest Destiny.

Over the past five years, the artists have explored various iterations of the project, and this volume is one manifestation, presented in conjunction with the exhibition at Dia Chelsea. In these pages, they have compressed the first twelve hours of recordings, from the Pacific to West Texas, into seventy-two minutes. Within these concentrated moments, voices largely from the present comment on a range of issues that resonate throughout the piece.

This publication and the exhibition it accompanies could not have happened without the dedication of numerous individuals. First and foremost, we are immensely grateful to artists Valeria Luiselli, Ricardo Giraldo, and Leo Heiblum, who have entrusted Dia with this work of art. It is an honor to serve as interlocutors with the artists over the past few years of development as well as to exhibit the work in progress and publish this chapbook. At Dia, Nathalie de Gunzburg Director Jessica Morgan as well as Ashanti Chaplin, Karey David, Alexis Lowry, Kelly Kivland, and Courtney Smith were early champions of the project. Ella den Elzen, Randy Gibson, Alexis Pennington-Foster, and John Sprague ably brought the exhibition to life. Karen Rasaby thoughtfully edited this volume designed by Laura Fields with great attunement to the artists' wishes. Meanwhile, David Morehouse and Karey David found crucial financial backing for both the show and book.

Echoes from the Borderlands is realized through a long-term partnership between Dia and the Institute for Studies on Latin American Art (ISLAA), and we remain grateful for ISLAA's vital support and collaboration. We are also thankful to the Economou Exhibition Fund for making possible all exhibitions at Dia.

1. Valeria Luiselli, "The Wild West Meets the Southern Border," *New Yorker*, June 3, 2019, https://www.newyorker.com/magazine/2019/06/10/the-wild-west-meets-the-southern-border.
2. Valeria Luiselli, *Lost Children Archive* (New York: Vintage Books, 2020), p. 55.
3. Valeria Luiselli, *Tell Me How It Ends: An Essay in Forty Questions* (Minneapolis: Coffee House Press, 2017), p. 30.
4. Valeria Luiselli, Ricardo Giraldo, and Leo Heiblum, in this volume, p. 31.

study one: call you when I get home

Use the QR code to connect to the corresponding audio track. Each of the following pages represents one minute, with time codes located at the outer margins, and is divided into three columns of text. The left column transcribes the voices of imagined personas, and the reader is encouraged to read their part aloud (see READER). The right column contains interviews, archival materials, and sound notations, the latter marked in color. The center column represents the underlying field recordings, indicated by geographical location, time of day, and microphones used.

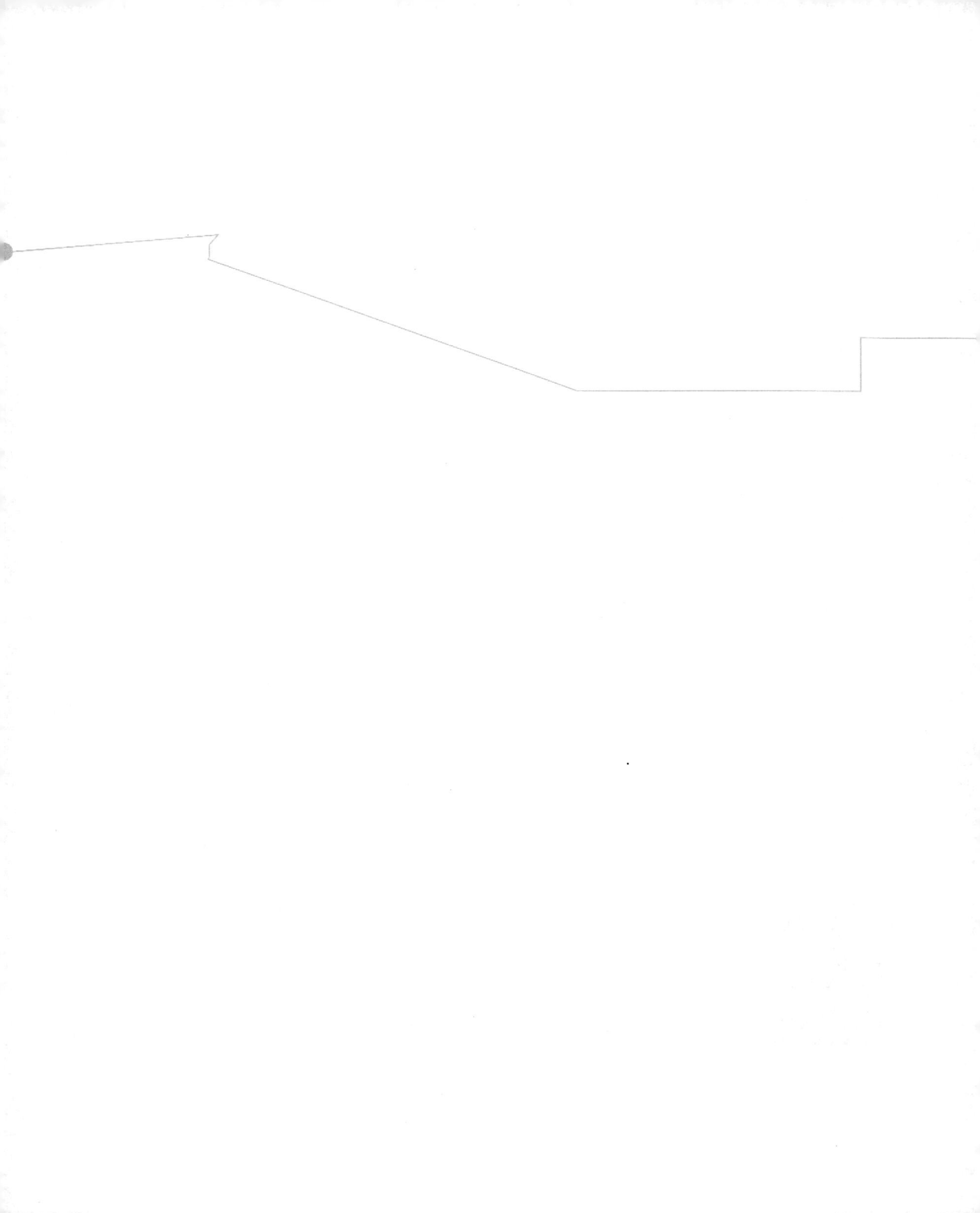

PACIFIC COAST, CA, 8:00 AM
HUMPBACK WHALE BIRTHING SEASON
HYDROPHONES UNDERWATER

BALLENAS [00.00.00]

( )
( )
( )
( )
( )
( )
( )
( )
( )
( )
( )
( )
( )
( )
( )
( )
( )
( )
( )
( )
( )
( )
( )
( )
( )
( )
( )
( )
( )

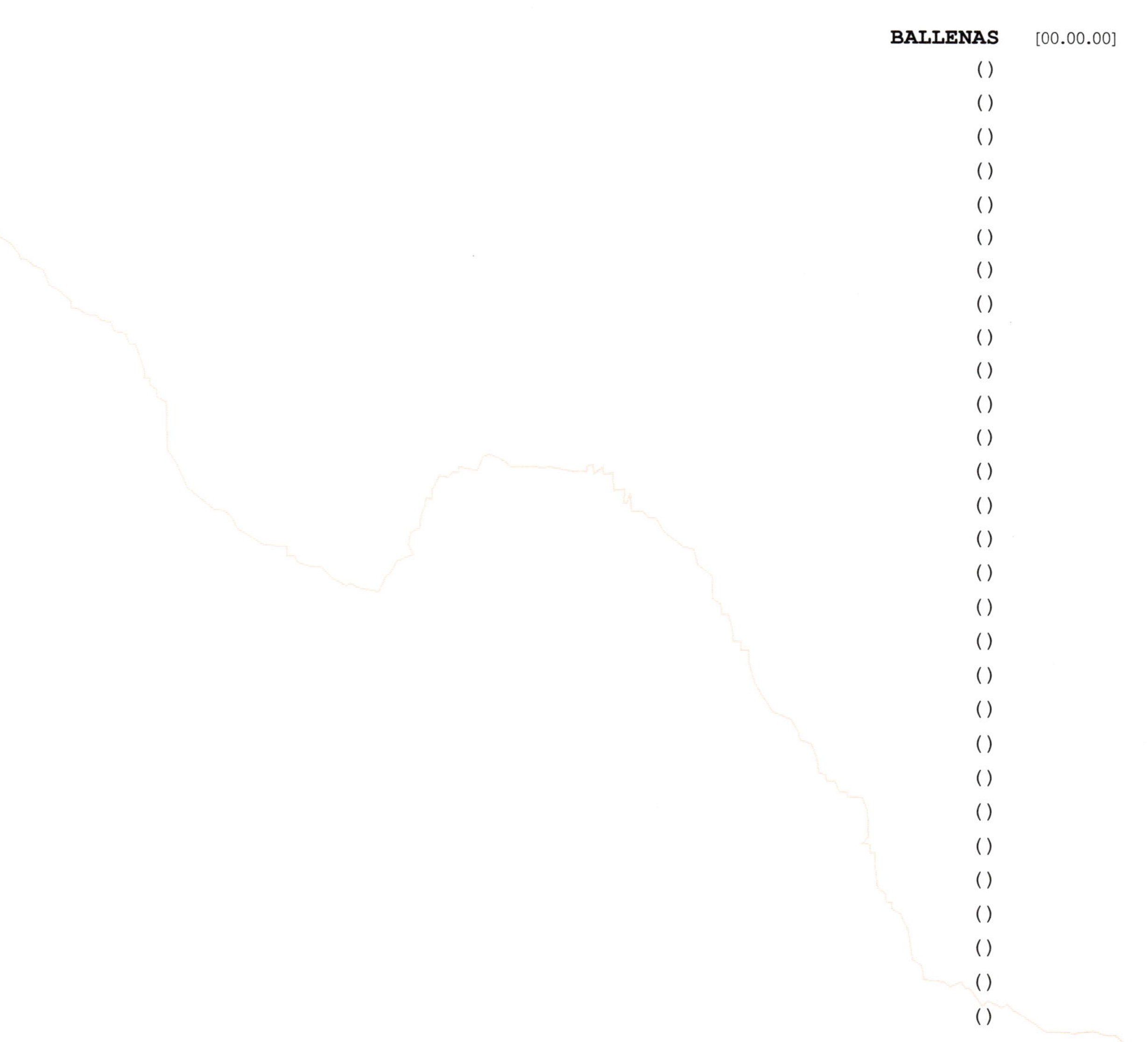

[00.01.15] entran olas

[00.01.20] **VOICE III**

I have a question:
In the beginning, in creation myths,
why are the earth and sky
always *cloven asunder*
and what does *cloven asunder*
really mean?

[00.01.33] **READER**

Partido en dos pedazos.

[00.01.41] **VOICE III**

And why are beginnings always torn apart?

[00.01.49] keys - water drops

And do things have to be broken to be told?

ANTHONY BELVADO [00.02.02]

This is during the flood.

VOICE III [00.02.10]

And once something is torn apart,
what is the rest of the story about?

READER [00.02.17]

A story not about
anything in particular
but a story with:
a story with copper,
barbed wire, walls, bombs,
but also rivers, and rocks,
and tongues, and land.

salen ballenas entran voces migra [00.02.37]

FRIENDSHIP PARK, CA, 8:25 AM
BEACH BORDER PATROL
QUAD AND BINAURAL MICS BY WALL

[00.03.10] **READER**

A la orilla, dos mitades.
Del lado de México, Playas de Tijuana.
Imperial Beach on the U.S. side.

[00.03.26] **BORDER PATROL**

... I've been learning from your ass.

[00.03.30] **READER**

We drive to Playas in a borrowed car
and drive right to the border,
almost right into the face
of the new wall.

[00.03.39] **VOICE II**

Steel bollards, eighteen feet high,
acned with oxide pustules
up and down their length.
Some bollards sprayed
with activist graffiti, some gently
brushstroked with hearts and flags,
some erased by the salty winds
that whip and erode.

[00.03.56] **VOICE III**

There are sweaters, ribbons, and shoes

tied around some steel bollards,
and on one bollard I saw a finger-painted
word and the word was *mamá*.

READER [00.04.10]

One shore cut in two
by two names
and a wall.

El muro raja la playa gris
y sigue y sigue,

and there, where the waves crash,
coiling into themselves,

the wall inserts itself in — olas más fuertes y viento [00.04.30]
the water like a sentence that
bends down,
bleeds down,
into the margin
of a page.

Steel bollards, eighteen feet high.

HOMBRE GARITA [00.04.50]

Call you when I get home.
...
Alright, I love you too.

[00.05.05] **VOICE II**

The first barrier was built by order of
President Truman, just after World War II:
Six miles of chain-link fence
—ten feet high, number six wire—
were dug up from the deserts where
Japanese Americans had been interned,
and the wires were driven south
and strung
between Calexico and Mexicali.
Each president has since potlucked
his bit of iron, steel, cement,
mesh, and wire.
Bush Father approved
fourteen miles parting the sprawl
of San Diego-Tijuana in two.
That fence was made with
helicopter-landing mats
repurposed from the Vietnam War.
Bill Clinton signed
Operation Gatekeeper,
Operation Hold the Line,
and Operation Safeguard,
and deployed Border Patrol
and surveillance like never before.
Bush Son funded seven hundred miles of wall:
steel tubes, reinforced with concrete,
twenty feet above the ground,
ten below the surface.

Barack Obama said no walls
but approved another hundred miles.
And Donald Trump
smiled for the camera,
        and pissed outside the hole.

MAIA [00.06.08]

Presidente! Presente?

VOICE III [00.06.13]

The new wall is lined with concertina,
which comes in long spools of coil
that can be expanded like an accordion.
It's oil-tempered, lined with razors,
and is much harder to cut
than ordinary barbed wire.
It was invented by the German
Horst Dannert in 1930-something:
a booming decade for wire.

READER [00.06.36]

We met some wall tourists once,
they were from Seattle,
had gone down to see their new wall.
Dismounting a big bike,
ankles swollen,
a lady stood right in front of it
and said: "Oh my oh my it's real!"—
like the sand that was real,
like the sun that was real,
like the sky that was an unbelievably
deep shade of blue.
She was impressed, she said.

Standing next to her
was her less impressionable
husband who explained—
well, he explained many things.

[00.07.08] **VOICE II**
And it's strange to think
that barbed comes from *barba*, beard,
and we're not certain but think
that the term *barbed* is indeed a
bearded form of wiring:
barbarum successit civilitas.

[00.07.20] **READER *allegro***
He explained:
"This is the point.
You see, this is how it works"
—larga barba parda, bandana y muñequeras—
and as he spoke,
describing how this new wall
keeps Mexicans out better, the beard
that spread, thick and slightly coiled,
from his chin and cheeks
[00.07.46] bobbled up and down, entra moto
in rhythm with the coils
of concertina grafted to the wall
that also bounced up and down.
Dusty wind gusts
whisk and spiral through it,
ráfagas polvosas, dusty wind gusts
[00.07.59] se arremolinan Apache violin

por el ducto en espiral.
Dusty gusts, but on the U.S. side,
larga barba parda and barbed wire,
gusts whisk, not the Mexican side,
whisk dust, not the Mexican side.

CAMINO DE LA PLAZA, CA, 9:21 AM
ROAD TRIP TO SAN YSIDRO
QUAD AND BINAURAL MICS INSIDE CAR

moto y Apache violin fade [00.08.16]

HOMBRE ZÓCALO [00.08.19]

Yo por tus papeles
no me quiero casar ...
Yo ya tengo viviendo aquí en tu país
como por más de tres cuatro años
y no necesito papeles.
Es la razón que me quiero casar contigo
es porque tú sabes y te consta
que la primera vez que te vi, me gustastes.
Ahora, ya tengo sentimientos por ti,
ya te quiero, y además ...
ya traes algo que me pertenece ...
Ya estaba embarazada.

HOMBRES GARITA [00.08.41]

Human
...
Pepto-Bismol
...
Motherfucker ...

FIESTA JARABE, CA, 9:30 AM
PEOPLE CROSSING BORDER
BINAURAL MIC ON PEDESTRIAN BRIDGE
QUAD MICS ON ACCESS RAMPS

[00.09.08]

MUJER GARITA

¿De dónde viene?

HOMBRE GARITA

De Tijuana.

MUJER GARITA

¡Oh! Vino a comprar y se va.

[00.09.25]

ruedas de maleta

[00.09.36]

HOMBRE ZÓCALO

Tons agarra y me dice ...
¿Tons no te quieres casar por papeles?
Nooo ...
¿Tú y tus papeles?
Es más, agarra tus papeles,
háztelos rollito y mételos por allá, le dije,
así le dije ... no mi amor.
Es más, te lo voy a comprobar.
Vamos a quedarnos juntos,
vamos a ver cuánto duramos juntos
sin casarnos. Ese fue un pretexto también,
porque yo tenía un dinero guardado
pa casarnos.

Pero era un pretexto
pa comprarme un Hondita,
que un güey me andaba vendiendo
en la chamba.
Agarré el dinero y me compré mi carrito.
Y así duramos,
como más de dieciocho o veinte años.

niño gritando córrele [00.10.16]

READER [00.10.17]

De un lado está Tijuana,
que se expande hasta topar con pared;
y del otro lado,
San Diego-Otay Mesa,
with its more angular grid.
At the foot of Otay Mountain,
where the outlets give way to scrap yards,
auto shops, and trucking facilities,
is a conglomerate
of prisons and detention centers.
The Otay Mesa Detention Center is there.

walkie-talkie [00.10.22]

OTAY MESA DETENTION CENTER, CA, 9:50 AM
PARKING LOT
QUAD AND BINAURAL MICS ON GROUND

MAIA [00.10.51]

Ahh ...
Because of the situations in their household

or war, gangs, and blah blah.
Like, you know what I mean?
So, a detention center is sort of like a jail
for children and adults and teenagers
where they keep the ...
They take apart the families
and send them to detention centers.

ELLA

Why?

MAIA

Because they are mean people.

ABUELA

But they are mean, the government, no?

MAIA

Sí, pero I want to explain this, plis!

MAMA

Yeah, we won't say anything, don't worry.

MAIA

So, they aks them questions
and they are very violent to them
and very rude and
so we actually don't really know
why they take them.
They just don't want them in their
in the U.S. ... place.

[00.11.50] **READER *allegro***

How do you explain that
"they just don't want them
in their U.S. place" means
keep them walled out, locked in,
and by all means
keep the women from having children.

Otay Mesa Detention Center ends [00.12.00]

VOICE II [00.12.02]

Early in the twentieth century,
in the name of eugenics
—"the science of improving stock" so as to
facilitate reproduction of
"more suitable races or strains of blood
over the less suitable ones"—
the United States became the first country
to enforce compulsory sterilization programs.
Women who were deemed
"feebleminded" were placed in institutions
and sterilized irreversibly,
in the name of eugenics.
California imposed
mandatory sterilization in 1909
and became the most efficient state
implementing eugenics laws;
it became the model for Nazi Germany's
racial-hygiene laws.

BOMBAY BEACH, CA, 10:07 AM
WIND IN WOODEN HOUSE
QUAD MICS ON BED
BINAURAL MIC IN LIVING ROOM

READER [00.12.50]

While California sterilized its women
(some of its women)
it intensively fertilized its land,
to the point of infertility.
And some of us would like to ask why.

And if we want to know why,
maybe the question is:
What questions should we ask?

And where should we look for answers?
Which street corners, which pairs of eyes,
which burning fields
or blue-green bodies of water?

We drive northeast from Otay
and into the Imperial Valley,
where in the early 1900s a company
created Calexico and Mexicali
for the purpose of encouraging settlement.

The speculators called Imperial Valley
a wasteland.

[00.13.41] crece viento

[00.13.44] **VOICE III**
But I want to know: Whose waste
[00.13.46] and whose land, keys - mosquito
Mr. Chairman of the Board?

[00.13.50] **READER**
They constructed irrigation canals
to divert water from the Colorado River
to the Salton Sink, an ancient lakebed
which was by then
a dried-up body of water.

They over-engineered it though,
se les pasó la mano,
and the Colorado swelled,
breached,
and eroded another two river courses.
        All the water flooded the valley.

A man-made cataclysm, a flood.
An entire river, trapped in a sink.

keys - fly [00.14.12]

CALIPATRIA, CA, 10:20 AM
NEAR ALGODONES DUNES
QUAD AND BINAURAL MICS ON ROAD

VOICE III [00.14.25]

The project was water:
water to turn the desert basin
into fertile land,
land for some to labor,
labor for some to birth,
labor for some to eat,
eat for some to grow,
grow for some to thrive,
thrive for some to rule,
rule for some to obey.

Obey your laws you say, Señores?
Same laws whatever name you give them:
eugenics, sanitation, population control,
immigration act.

Dam the river, sterilize the women,
seize the land, and take the water.

[00.15.02] **SEMICHORUS**

Don't take the water, take the water.

[00.15.04] **BOMBAY BEACH PROMO**

Water ...
Water has changed the face of the desert,
and it's made the lands so fertile
that anything grows here:
carrots, dates, onions, lettuce,
grapefruit, oranges, lemons,
just to name a few.

This land brings a higher gross return
for agricultural acreage
than any land in the nation,
and there is water
for home and industry.

And naturally, in the golf capital of the world,
there has to be water for the golf courses.

There are thirty-seven golf courses
in this area alone.

And another kind of water
has been added to the desert

that was never planned,
never dreamed of:
recreation water,
the vast Salton Sea.
385 square miles of water
formed by accident back in 1905
when the Colorado River ran wild
over man-made dikes.
A sea in the desert
with its wide sandy beaches.
No tides
or dangerous undercurrents.

... and with literally millions of fish
ready for the taking.

VOICE II [00.16.35]

California was responsible
for one third of all forced sterilizations.
All the fish ready for the taking

promo music ends [00.16.44]

SEMICHORUS

CHORUS [00.16.55]

Desalinating it, channeling it,
tubing it,

piping it, just imagine it.

A hysterectomy

to remove the womb,
and usually the cervix, too.

A tubal ligation,

Channeling it,
way beyond,
    just imagine it.
Desalinating it, channeling it,
    just imagine it.

the tubes are cloven asunder
    and the skin incision
is stitched closed.

[00.17.17] **VOICE III**
Imagine the pipes and lines:
2.6 million miles of pipelines,
twisted and untwisted fallopians,
under the body of the United Estates.

[00.17.28] **VOICE II**
Strange that *sterilize* should mean
both *clean* and *make infertile*.
And strange, that *labor* should mean
[00.17.35] both *give birth* and *work*,
like the animal laborans we are,
in a series of continuous,
progressive, painful,
physical and social
contractions of the uterus
used to produce goods and services
that help the cervix dilate and efface,
in the service of the economy,
whereby the fetus moves through
the birth canal.

Ana pariendo

READER *allegro molto* [00.18.00]

Extraño que *labor* se refiera al parto
pero también al trabajo,
y que el parto sea partir:
irse y partirse en dos.
Y que las manos mexicanas trabajen
para que las bocas gringas coman
y que los mexicanos se vayan, se partan,
se partan en dos y se partan la madre
y que a las madres mexicanas
les sea negado el derecho a parir.

DOLORES HUERTA [00.18.16]

Support has been highlighted
by people who have joined us here today.
Furthermore, these groups
are committing themselves
to help us
until total victory is achieved.
The developments of the past seven months
are only a slight indication of what is to come.
The workers are on the rise.
There will be strikes all over the state
and throughout the country,
because Delano has shown what can be done
and the workers know
that they are no longer alone.
Sí se puede
Sí se puede
Sí se puede
...

CALEXICO BORDER, CA, 11:10 AM
KIDS PLAYING BASKETBALL
QUAD MICS ON CAR WHEELS
BINAURAL MIC ON CAR ROOF

[00.19.11]

BASKETBOLERO

I was getting it back ...

[00.19.14]

basketball mashup

[00.19.30]

FRED MOTEN

The mountain is not a place,

the mountain is a practice.

The Earth is moving, right?
It it it it goes against ...
you understand?
It's against the grain
of the simplistic modalities
of global positioning, right?
That actually constitute
the geographic foundations
of settler colonialism.

You can't settle the Earth,
motherfucker,

cause the Earth is in motion.

You can't settle the Earth, motherfucker.

It, it ...
we inhabit that movement,
and that places an ethical responsibility on us.
You don't stomp all over something
when it's moving.
You don't plant flags on it.
You rightly step with it,
in rhythm with it,
in rhythm with it, right?
You look with it, not at it.
You move with it,
in rhythm with it.

NATALIE DIAZ [00.20.46]

If they can take it,
what knowledge is
based on,
if they can take it.
...
The people who try to extract them,
don't understand them.

[00.21.00]

FRED MOTEN

The mountain is not a place,

the mountain is a practice.

The mountain is not a place,

the mountain is a practice.

You can't settle the Earth, motherfucker,
cause the Earth is in motion.
In rhythm with it,
in rhythm with it,
right?

You can't settle the Earth,
motherfucker.

[00.21.40] road trip

[00.21.55] **READER**

Under a full moon in the coldest month,
around the year 1450
in Hohokam land, on a mountain,
desert humidity levels rose above average,
and the night was still.

YUMA PROVING GROUND, AZ, 11:50 AM
INTERSTATE 8, CARS DRIVING EAST
QUAD AND BINAURAL MICS IN ROADWAY MEDIAN

READER [00.22.16]

A splash of lichen,
slow and small and yellow,
on the surface of a red rock,
completed an expansion cycle.
And next to that rock, a new saguaro
pushed out of the ground
just enough
to crack the crust of earth above it.

VOICE III [00.22.28]

And which story do you believe in?

READER [00.22.35]

The saguaro,
  some people believed,
was a little girl
who had disappeared
into a hole
in the ground.

ELIJAH [00.22.50]

Nobody listening,
nobody has time to listen.

[00.23.24] **VOICE III**

After the great flood
the mountain opened its mouth
   and the people came out.

[00.23.41] motorbike passes

[00.23.43] **READER**

Thick storm clouds gather
above the mountain
and cover the enormous granite peak,
and the rain will come down lightly

where the mountain is a practice,
and not pierce the earth
where the mountain is a word
and the mountain is a mountain.

CHORUS [00.24.00]

This is the story of the missing,
the missing story.
This is our voice,
the voice that misses.
These are our bodies
and this in our hand
is a wet round rock.

KIM [00.24.15]

You can't see the mountain,
Baboquivari mountain, but that's I'itoi
and he's our creator, yeah,
and he sits up there and watches and he just,
I guess, supposedly guides us through life.
And like you see the man in the maze
and that's the whole purpose, is
where you walk and you go through
and that's your life journey,
you know, everything happens for a reason.
And you follow that path,
and that's different for everybody,
and then at death is when you
you reach the center, I guess.

CHORUS ECHO [00.24.54]

And this in our hand
is a wet round rock.

GILA RIVER, AZ, 12:10 PM
WIND THROUGH LEMON TREES
QUAD MICS AROUND TREE
BINAURAL MIC BETWEEN TREE LINES

[00.25.25]

MAIA

And what happened next?

[00.25.26]

ANTHONY BELVADO

I did what he told me to do.
What was missing.
So, I went back to him
and I told him the problem,
and he just had a big smile
and he just broke out laughing.
The Apache people
have a way of teaching you,
instructing you.
They leave things out.
And he told me
what was missing.

[00.25.58]

Bombay Beach wind
whistling and chorus echo

ANTHONY [00.26.00]

( )

( )

( )

( )

BERTHA [00.26.12]

Ok, I'm gonna tell you something.
Back in the old San Carlos,
you know,
us people arrived from there,
in the old San Carlos.
And ever since
then we've
kind of moved to
different areas,
you know,
so, people live
here and there.
My father was
a
should I say
...
a medicine man,
and he did
a lot of folklores,
a lot of stories, folklores ...
He told
a lot of stories.

Anthony's song [00.26.58]

[00.27.04]

BERTHA

Around the curve right there,
something whistled at us.
()
It was a mountain lion
that whistled at us
and he was standing there.
Where is it?
Where is it?
Now hurry up, come on
let's go!
Because it might just jump on you,
you know,
but anyways ...
...
Back in the days,
to-ni-ra,
the little people
()
()
()
()
I can take you guys up there.
They come down this way,
you know.
Looking for water,
food,
and this and that.

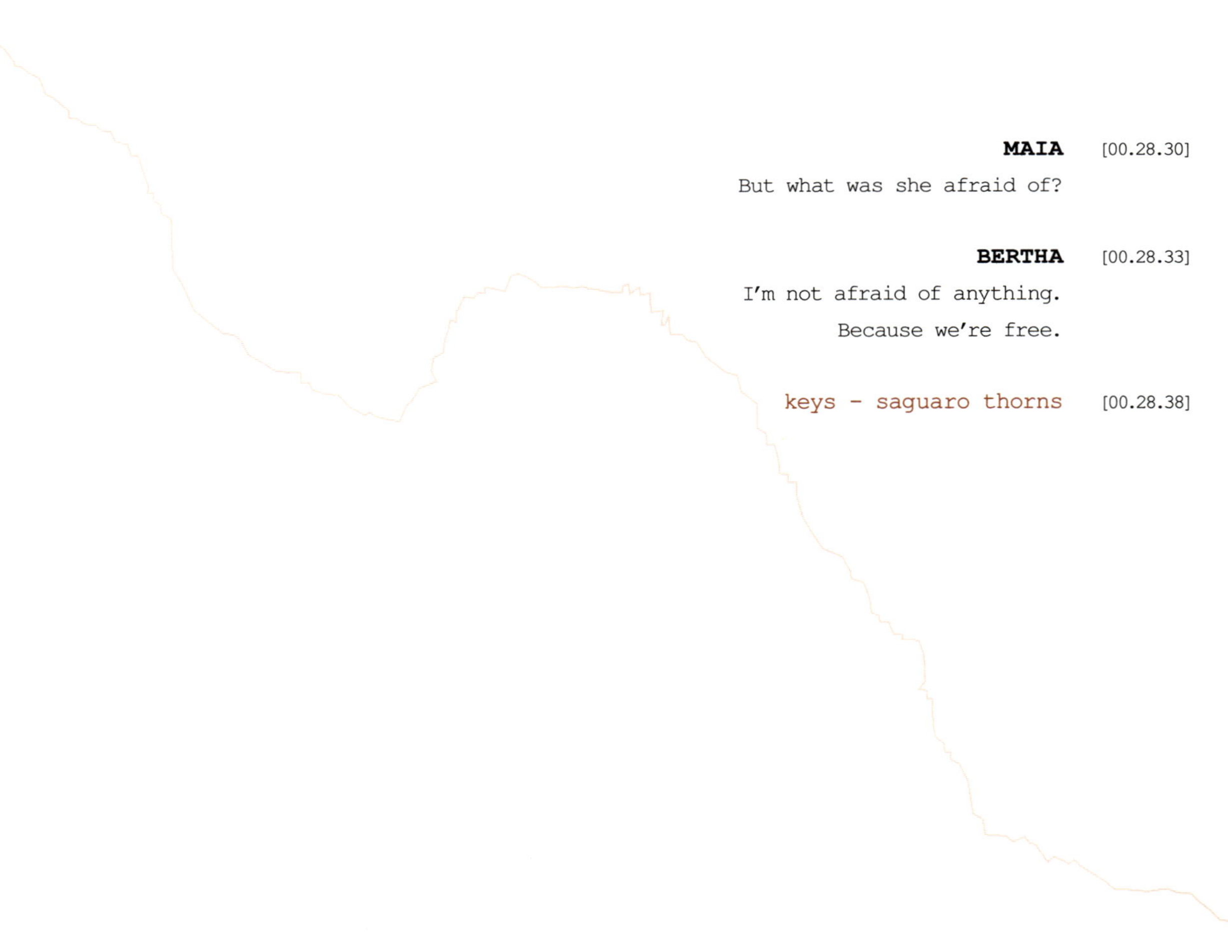

MAIA [00.28.30]

But what was she afraid of?

BERTHA [00.28.33]

I'm not afraid of anything.
Because we're free.

keys - saguaro thorns [00.28.38]

[00.29.30]

ANTHONY BELVADO

I believe there are
little people here.
Like everywhere else.
I hear stories
of people seeing them
and, I guess, in a way
make contact with them.
But they are here.

Like everything else,
everything is here.

[00.29.49]

jarana

READER [00.30.06]

This is the story of the missing,
the missing story.

But how do you listen to what is missing?

How do you document what is not there?

VOICE III [00.30.21]

Maybe you don't.
Maybe you just make space.

jarana [00.30.30]

NATALIE DIAZ [00.30.39]

When I'm thinking about,
you know,
ideas of translation, I'm thinking a lot,
like many of us are, about knowledge;
what is knowledge, who determines
the value of knowledge,
and once that value is determined,
who then determines how it is disseminated
and to whom it's disseminated.
And for me thinking of knowledge as ...

I mean the way knowledge exists ...
I think it's the very nature of the word
—it's a word I don't trust—
the very nature of the word
implies that it can be extracted.
It can be consumed.
It can be again made sense of,
and it can be made
to have value.
Because we live in America,
because the power of
Western structures
of democracy,
of empire, of nation,
government,
all of these things,

because they have
created this system
in which they decide
what knowledge is ...
based on
if they can take it, right?
So, Indigenous bodies of knowledge
—Indigenous knowledge systems—
they are so important
to resist
what is academic knowledge
or these many centers of knowledge,

because ...

because they're knowledges
that can't be taken,
and they can't be taken
because the people who try to extract them
from the communities
don't understand them.

talking door and bees [00.32.14]

keys - saguaro thorns [00.32.55]

[00.33.10] **READER**

One morning,
in Hohokam land,
the year 2020,
a blast.
7 am, five yellow bulldozers rolled in,
metal blades
pushing sand
and rocks.

Behind the wheel of one of the bulldozers
a man, almost a boy,
chewing blueberry chewing gum,
drove to the cusp of a hill
and adjusted his hat, and just as he
struck the saguaro
he received a text message from his girlfriend:
"Not pregnant. See you tonight?"
He felt its resistance when he drove over it
but didn't see it falling,
didn't hear it, either,
the more than nine hundred thorns,
in domino, piercing the ground,
two strabic arms hitting the sand and
simply snapping off the torso of the
six-ton green beast,
hissing, crying, breaking:
No one recorded any sound.

VOICE III [00.34.00]

The sound of things falling,
a world disappearing.

fireworks [00.34.18]

REENACTOR [00.34.19]

It's really not a hard job at all.
Probably, the most difficult part
would probably be trying to
be keeping up with ammo production.
I make the ammo,
I make the ammo
and I've got my helpers.
William right over here helps me out.
Just anybody on the ... can do ammos
as long as I trained them properly.
First part is probably making sure
you have clean shells.
We use forty-five shells
and then you have to prime 'em.
Then you gotta pack them
with gunpowder and
something called vermiculite.
Vermiculite is just there
to keep the powder inside the gun
and make it boom.
It's about forty dollars for a pound of primer,
five dollars for vermiculite,
huge bag of vermiculite.
Your shells are probably
your most expensive, probably,

about a buck and a half a shot.

[00.35.01] saloon music

[00.35.28] **VOICE III**

Remember when I asked you:
Why are the earth and sky
always *cloven asunder*?

[00.35.33] inside car

[00.35.40] **VOICE I**

Always gold, always what they wanted
in Spain was gold.
Los cartógrafos dibujaron un contorno
lo llamaron el Despoblado.
        The Unpeopled.
But the Despoblado estaba lleno:
        adobe, mesquite,
saguaros, cepillo sabio, yuca.
        Y voces:
Piro, Tiwa, Tewa, Keres, Jemez,
Zuni, Navajo, Apache, Maricopa,
Yuma, Mohave, Yavapai, Walapai.

ANTHONY BELVADO [00.36.00]

Back in the 1800s,
when the Apaches were here,
they controlled all of Arizona,
New Mexico, part of Texas, and
this was their land.

inside car, fireworks, birds [00.36.20]

[00.37.00]

PÁJARO

( )

( )

( )

( )

( )

GERONIMO TRAIL, AZ, 2:12 PM
BORDER WALL, OPEN DOORS
QUAD AND BINAURAL MICS FACING WALL

[00.37.28]

DOUG

It's a hole,
a very large hole.
It's cone shaped, ok?
And what they've done in the mining of it
is they've started wide at the top and
they're starting to cone downward, and
they are taking it in layers
and the layers are fifty feet apart.
And as it cuts through it,
it cuts through different rock layers,
so you get these vibrant colors
like kind of a purplish red,
a lavender color,
even though it's not named after lavender.
You'll have these grays,

reds, and greens,
and in the bottom of it you'll find these ...
During the rainy season, the monsoons,
the pools of water will turn bright green,
almost black and green.
But currently I think all that is down
there is bright,
dark, rusty red colored pools
going to black.

READER *adagio molto* [00.38.20]

The first time I saw an open-pit copper mine
was in Bisbee, Arizona.

It made me nauseous, dizzy, sick:
the copper,
the pit, the sick.

CHRIS [00.38.38]

It's just like any place else in America,
there's no difference,
there's nothing distinctive
in that way.
But if you look at it,
the reality today:
it's the blast zone.
It's the after of
two hundred years of extreme

colonization.
This whole area was called
the internal colony.

[00.39.06] **READER**

El cuenco de la mina es rojo y hondo,
excavado en una serie de cortes abruptos,
escalonados, como las antiguas terrazas
de cultivo en las laderas de las montañas;
pero en vez de cultivos de cebada y trigo,
el terraceado de la mina de cobre
—arena sobre roca sobre arena—
desciende en espiral yermo
y se detiene súbitamente
en un ojo de agua negra.

[00.39.35] **DOUG**

Bright, dark, rusty red colored pools
going to black.

[00.39.40] ambiente denso y grave en mina

[00.39.42] **CHORUS**

This is the story of the missing
...
is a wet round rock.

[00.39.52] **DOUG**

These mines will burn the rock.
Long rods of rock.

[00.39.54] **VOICE II**

The oldest metals known to humans
—human hands plus human imagination,

machination—
are gold, silver, then copper.
In the genealogy of the IUD,
the three metals made lineage:
gold, silver, then copper,
in that order.
Except the first IUD.
The first one was invented
in Germany in 1909,
by a man called Richard Richter.
It was made of silkworm gut
and was unpopular.
Then came Ernst Gräfenberg,
also German,
who in 1929
invented a device made of silver.
Gräfenberg had done research
about female ejaculation,
which later led
to the conceptualization
and coining of the term *G-spot*—
an accomplishment more
in lexicon than in
empirical knowledge, for most men.
But the point is,
Gräfenberg's silver IUD
was short-lived
because he was Jewish
during the Nazi regime.
So, before he fled the country,

they had already banned
his contraceptive method,
saying it was a threat to Aryan women
(they meant: threat to nonreproductive
copulation, to sex just for play and pleasure,
a promise of pleasure for women in general,
therefore a threat to Aryan men in particular
but also men in general).

[00.41.20] **DOUG**

We are from here.
We've been here since 1883, ok?

[00.41.24] mine train

SEMICHORUS

This is the story of the missing,
the missing story.
This is our voice, the voice that misses.

These are our bodies
and this in our hand
is a wet round rock.

CHORUS [00.42.00]

This is the story of the missing,
the missing story.
This is our voice, the voice that misses.

These are our bodies
and this in our hand
is a wet round rock.

READER [00.42.35]

From high above,
standing behind a mesh fence
from where the full extent
of the quarry is visible,
I looked down
into the open-pit copper mine,
observed that hole at its center
full of black water,
and tried hard to imagine,
made an effort to understand:

What drives men to dig
and dig further?

[00.43.02] **SEMICHORUS**

DOUG

These mines will burn the rock.

This is the story of the missing.

Long rods of rock,

These are our bodies

really pretty rocks.

I was a kid when the mine shut down.

and this in our hand is a wet round rock.

[00.43.20] **MAIA**

Geology is all about rocks and drift, therefore
extraction, therefore
chain gangs, therefore
forced relocation, therefore
dispossession, therefore
displacement, therefore
drift and rocks.

[00.43.44] **DOUG**

First thing you do is
you need to locate a deposit, ok?
And then,
you can just suspect that it's there.
In the modern world
you are going to use geophysics, ok?
And just ... it's basic geology,
and then
you are going to take core samples.
Just, you know,

drill down and take,
you know, long rods of rock, and
then you are going to ...
If you hit something unusual
you are going to take assays
and then determine the metal.
And then you say "oh, we hit some copper here"
and this one roll,
we'll draw a series of holes around it, to uh ...
and then you take samples of it all
and then you basically connect the dots, ok?
A three-dimensional
connect-the-dots, ok?
We got copper here, here, and here,
so you get the idea of the shape of that.
And then to see you've got one of those
masses of copper over here,
and at five hundred feet away you got another one,
and then your engineers
will actually draw ...
design a pattern of tunnels,
they're like building roads, ok?
Like connecting cities.
And the miners will come in
and they'll drive the tunnels
to go mine those ore bodies.
Now generally you are ...
you are going to start below the ore and
then you are going to take slices, take cuts,
and you are gonna work up on the ore.
Usually in Bisbee

there are like big blobs, ok.

[00.45.03] **CHRIS**

We live in the blast zone.

[00.45.04] **DOUG**

Big blobs ... Big blobs
Bisbee ... Bisbee ... Bisbee

[00.45.08] **VOICE II**

Later, in 1934, a Japanese doctor,
Dr. Ota, developed an IUD made of gold.
It was called the Pressure Ring—
a name that has something
of *engagement*
and something of *corset*.
It didn't last, so, end of story.

Finally in the 1960s, a gringo
doctor named Howard Tatum
invented a device
in the shape of a T.
He thought a T would better adjust
to the uterus.
He partnered with a Chilean doctor,
Dr. Zipper, who in turn discovered
that copper was an effective spermicide
and could be added
to the plastic skeleton
of the T-shaped device.

It is possible, though this is not something
confirmed by any source whatsoever,

that that same Dr. Zipper
is related to the inventor
of the mechanism by which
little metal teeth
hook into little metal hollows,
aligned in a ladder pattern
and pressed into each other by a slide that
glides up and down that ladder,
the whole thing a mere means
to the end of opening and closing, zipping,
unzipping the boundary
—cotton, denim, polyester—
that divides our naked bodies
from the outside world; flies, especially.

DOUG [00.46.31]

I absolutely love to drill.

silence [00.46.34]

READER [00.46.38]

What drives men to dig?
Carve their way in,
deeper and deeper.

DOUG [00.46.46]

It's a lot of physical work,
but it's very very peaceful, ok?
To become ...
When you are drilling,
just stay out of trouble, ok?
You need to block out the world,
it's almost like you are Zenning out,

and you just focus on the drill, ok?
And you're paying attention to the slight changes
and vibrations of the drill,
the sound of the drill,
and the water coming out of the hole.
Because when these are showing and you are
going through different rock types and
you feel the drill, then you can change this,
you need to slow the drilling down
and when it gets consistent again
you speed it back up, yeah,
and that keeps you from sticking your drill
in steel, stuff like that, yeah.
I love it, yeah, drilling is great.
It's so peaceful, it really is.
A lot of work but it's peaceful.

[00.47.36] **READER**

Dig and dig further—
to find what?

A gleam,
a promise,
matter with specific mass.

Something to inject energy into,
with anger or with pain,
drill into it, hammer it,
blast it; have it, take it.

Something to have
and eventually trade,

something to defend
and wage wars for,
establish settlements around,
found a company and then
name a town
that might maybe spread around it;
pick a president,
designate positions, accountants,
secretaries and undersecretaries;
build an industry; promise partners,
shares, and heirs, fortunes;
dig deeper and dig more, multiplying the
enslaved and indentured hands
of men who drink weak coffee
before daybreak
and then too much mean alcohol
after the day's work.

MAIA [00.48.06]

Chairmen of the board!

keys - gaita transformador [00.48.10]

VIVIR QUINTANA [00.48.34]

Aaaaaaaaaaaaaaaaa
La pinche jornada laboral larga.
Pinche jornada larga.
Pinche larga la,
pinche.

NACO, AZ, 4:10 PM
BORDER WALL, HELLS ANGELS
QUAD AND BINAURAL MICS INSIDE CAR

[00.49.00] **READER**

Una y otra vez porque
nunca se pinche acaba,
      it's never fucking over
      whatever they name it:
oro para el emperor,
búsqueda de plata,
Operation Gatekeeper,
Removal Act, national security,
war on drugs,
       zero tolerance.

()
()
()
()
()
()

[00.49.40] **TREN**

()
()
()
()
()
()
()
()
()
()
()
()
()
()

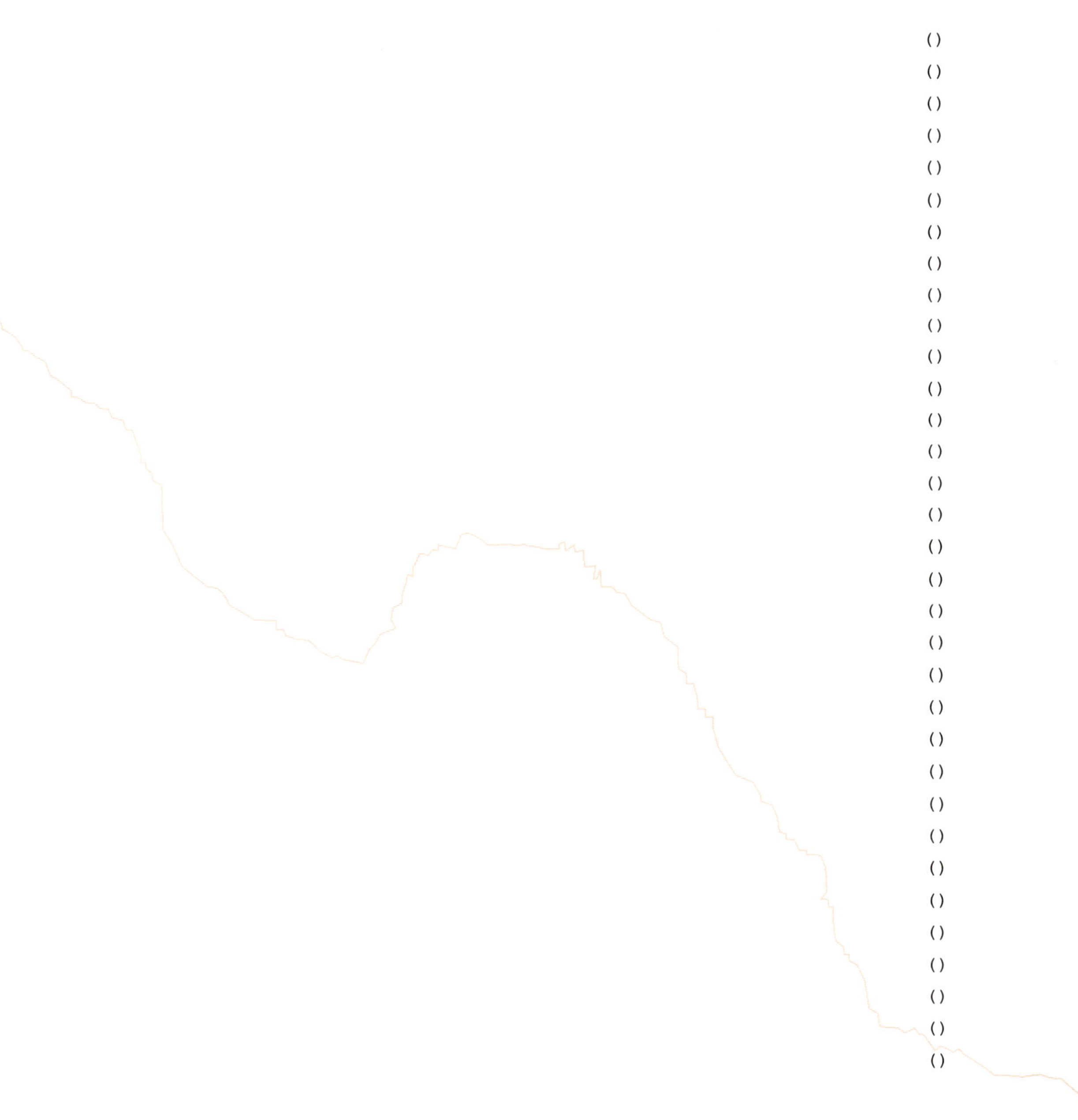

BOWIE, AZ, 4:40 PM
UNION PACIFIC TRAIN PASSING
QUAD AND BINAURAL MICS BY TRAIN TRACKS

()
()
()
()
()
()
()
()
()
()
()
()
()
()
()
()
()
()
()
()
()
()
()
()
()
()
()
()
()
()
()

()

()

()

tren ends [00.52.10]

CHIRICAHUA MOUNTAINS, AZ, 4:41 PM
ECHO CANYON
QUAD AND BINAURAL MICS IN RAVINES

Chiricahua echoes "perdón" [00.52.20]

Johnny Bones [00.52.24]
Chiricahua stream

keys - mining transformer [00.52.42]
inside Copper Queen Mine

ANTHONY BELVADO [00.52.55]

()

()

( )
( )
( )
( )
( )
( )
( )
( )
( )
( )
( )
( )
( )
( )
( )
( )
( )
( )
( )
( )
( )
( )
( )
( )
( )
( )
( )
( )
( )
( )
( )

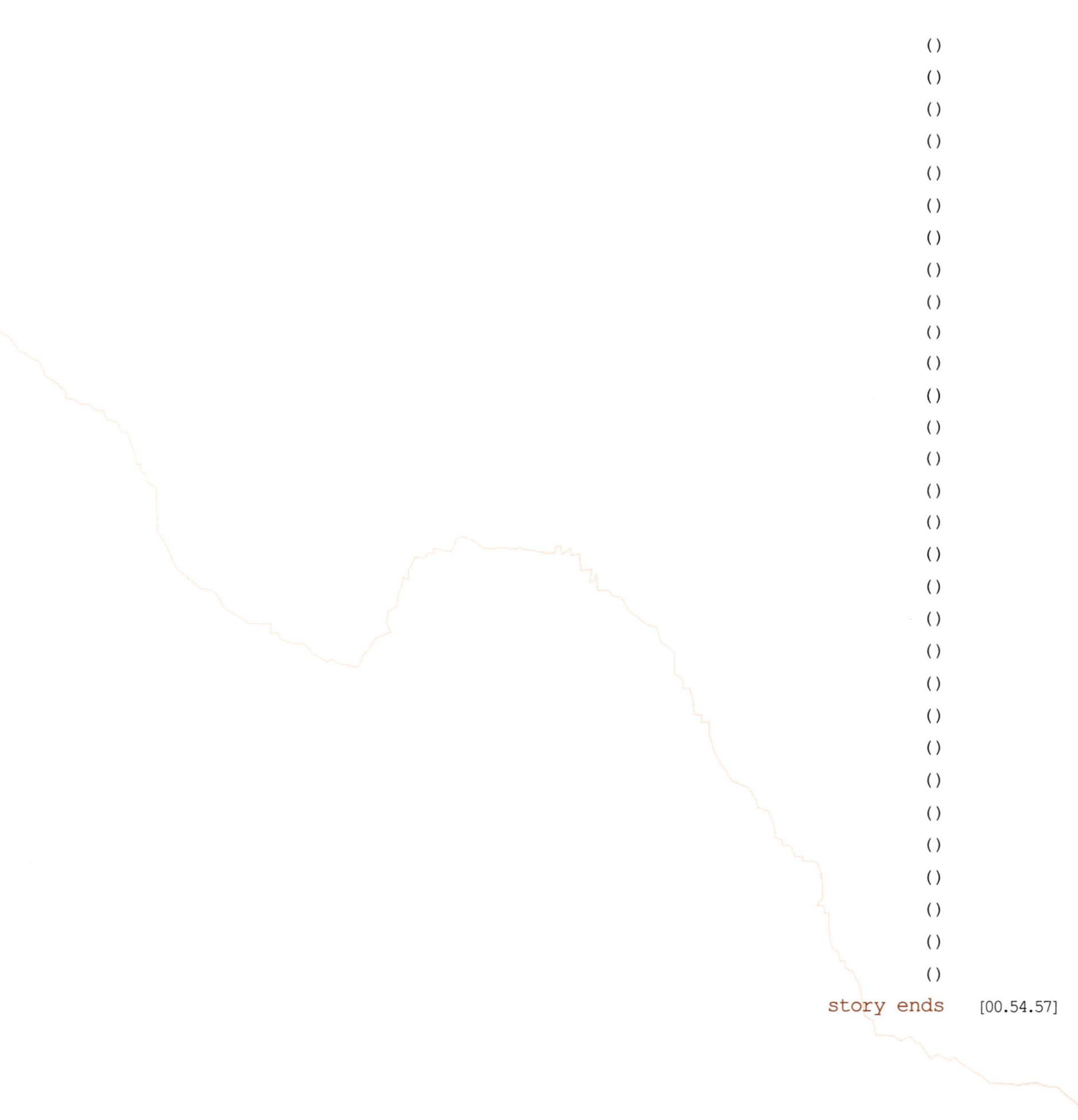

()
()
()
()
()
()
()
()
()
()
()
()
()
()
()
()
()
()
()
()
()
()
()
()
()
()
()
()
()
()

story ends [00.54.57]

[00.55.40] clap

[00.55.41] **VALERIA**

But don't forget
what you were about to say
because it sounded like
we were going somewhere good.
So, we are in Santa Fe,
New Mexico.
Today is May 22
of the year 2022
and we are
speaking with Arte.
Last name, Arte?

ARTE (ANA) [00.56.04]

Romero y Carver.
Alright, let's do it.

One day all the cops evaporated.
Not just their bodies
but their uniforms and their badges.
Exhausted of being part
of the construction of an officer,
every single particle got up and left.
The particles wanted to do something useful
so they became water.
When the snow melted, the Rio Grande grew
and ran like a kid in the summer.
During the monsoon season,
we opened tarp flowers
and built more gutters.
And then, once we got rid
of iodine in Brita filters,
we drank the police and
we irrigated them
into corns and beans and squash,
and on hot days, families and kids played
in their melted authority.
And when the wildfires came,
burning into family homes,
the police condensed and fell as rain
and people joked that for the first time ever
they had actually protected us.
Somewhere on the East Coast
the *New York Times* published an article

about reforming the water cycle.
Somewhere on a morning with
a Bluetooth speaker playing in the shower,
I am washing my hair with Officer Ramírez,
with Officer Ramírez.

[00.57.14] **MAIA**
I just have one question.

[00.57.20] **ARTE**
People joked they had actually protected us.

[00.57.24] **MAIA**
I ... just ... have ... one ... question.

[00.57.30] **READER**
¿A qué le tienes miedo?

[00.57.33] **MARTA**
Perder claridad.

[00.57.36] **READER**
What are you afraid of?

[00.57.38] **VOICE II**
I'm afraid of forgetting,
of things being forgotten.

[00.57.43] **MAIA**
Well, I don't know
what I'm afraid of.

[00.57.55] **VOICE III**
I'm afraid of the Earth burning, flooding,
afraid of catastrophes.

MILITARY AIRPLANE [00.58.00]

()

JOEY [00.58.08]

Time to get sick.

READER [00.58.12]

I’m afraid of losing my loved ones.

MESCALERO, NM, 5:50 PM
SAINT JOSEPH APACHE MISSION
QUAD MICS BETWEEN PEWS
BINAURAL MICS IN AISLE

MILITARY AIRPLANE [00.58.30]

()

()

()

()

()

()

()

()

()

()

()

()

()

()

()

()

()

()

()

[00.59.15] **VOICE III**

Long ago, probably not long
after the beginning and
the cleaving asunder and the flood,
an ancient sea covered
most of the Southwest.
Layers of gypsum
deposited on the seafloor
for years and years.
Over time, the ancient sea
slowly retreated,
tectonic plates collided then parted,
vast rift zones spread between them,
some land flattened in arid valleys
some rose in narrow-faulted
mountain chains,
animals and plants metamorphosized,
lakes appeared then disappeared.
Gods died and were forgotten.

Then, the geologists came along.
[00.59.49] The geologists had long robes ballenas
and pens and mathematics,
and terms like *rift*.

MAIA [01.00.02]

Geology is about rocks and drift.

READER [01.00.15]

In the middle of the rift zone,
in what is now New Mexico,
the Tularosa Basin
spread wide and white.
And there, entre los cerros tupidos
de los Apaches Mescaleros,
and the juniper, pines, and aspens
of the Gila Forest,
laboratories flowered,
and military bases followed,
and concrete was poured
for landing strips,
and barbed wire marked new limits,
and the basin was declared
a proving ground:
a ground to confirm, convince,
determine, substantiate,

and test.

DEMETRIA MARTINEZ [01.00.52]

... upon which the bomb ticked
toward its destiny:
5.29 and 45 seconds am
mountain war time.

The words
mushroom cloud
did justice to the explosion's
lush appearance.
On my way back to the gate
I searched the ground for Trinitite.
The glassy green particles came into being
when the heat of the bomb
congealed steel and desert sand.
The fragments are like something
you would buy at a bead show
to make jewelry out of,
except that they are radioactive.

[01.01.30]

JOEY

Violence is always gonna be there,
you know.
But it will always be
around us,
all the time,
it's never gonna end.

They put us in prisons,
gave us spoiled meat and
all that stuff to feed us.

They took ...

They tried to starve us,
away from the mescal,

the buffalo.
I mean, you know,
a lot of it,
it don't work though.

READER [01.02.10]

We drive to the White Sands Missile Range;
once an ocean, now
a test-bombing site.
A sign says: "Birthplace of America's
Missile and Space Activity."
The army has tested more than
forty thousand missiles and rockets here.
We don't have U.S. passports
so the soldier at the checkpoint tells us
we are not allowed in
but are welcome to visit the dunes,
just a few miles further,
mostly open to visitors
(only closed during missile testing).
"Just remember sunblock and hats
and maybe buy some sleds at a dollar store,
because the powdery white sand dunes look
and behave like snow," and indeed,
when we pull over in front of a blinding
white mass of pulverized gypsum,
there are entire families sliding down
humps and slopes
on plastic snow saucers.

[01.03.04] children playing

[01.03.12] **READER**
White Sands stretches for 150 miles or so,
exactly in line with the majestic
Sacramento Mountains—next to
the Mescalero Apache Reservation—
where the army has tested more than
forty thousand missiles and rockets.

[01.03.49] pelotazo, silence

[01.03.53] **VOICE III**
In mythology and geology,
in endings and beginnings,
things are always being
rifted apart,
and no one here seems
to know why.

READER [01.04.05]

I don't have a theory,
I don't know what to say;
chaos they say,
cosmos they say.

What should we say, in the way
of beginning and ending?
I don't know what to say.

LINCOLN NATIONAL FOREST, NM, 6:32 PM
HUMMINGBIRDS FLYING
QUAD AND BINAURAL MIC ON DECK

JOEY [01.04.23]

And night became day.
They didn't tell us nothing.
You gotta realize that it's army,
military,
so they don't have to tell you anything,
you understand?
And they don't,
they do what they want.

READER *allegro* [01.04.45]

He flies his slightly curved open palm
over his wooden desk, White Sands
just next to the Mescalero Reservation,
his slightly curved open palm
over his desk from the dunes
into the mountains.

[01.05.00]

JOEY

We used to have parrots here and
palm trees here,
like Mexico.
When they let that bomb go,
it all died.
The first thing that went
was the birds,
and then the trees,
and then cancer
came in.
Smallpox came in,
our immunities went down
in all of us.
So when the smallpox came,
it killed a lot of our people.

Malaria came here,
killed a lot of our people also.

We deal with cancer a lot here now,
before we didn't have that,
until they let that bomb go.

[01.05.50] **READER**

They detonated
the atomic bomb
(just for practice they said)
in the long
white plains
of New Mexico.

JOEY [01.06.05]

Night became day,
everything started dying around us.
It shook the earth,
they felt it.

ballenas [01.06.08]

READER [01.06.25]

And where are we now?
What is the shape of *unthinkable*
and *unimaginable*?

JOEY [01.06.30]

Because they used it on Japan,
but also they used it on us too.
Like when the jets
start flying around here,
my grandmother
used to always tell us
"Time to get sick"
(time to get sick).
You understand me?
And it's still happening
to this day,
they experiment on
a lot of Indians.
They don't have to tell you.

So that's what my grandma
used to always tell me,
"Well, time to get sick now."

LINCOLN NATIONAL FOREST, NM, 7:45 PM
QUAD MICS AROUND TREE
BINAURAL MICS BETWEEN TREES

[01.07.15] **READER**

And where are we now?
And how do we dwell?
And what longing is this?

[01.07.35] **VOICE III**

Maybe in another beginning
the ancient sea will come back,
and the waters from the Pacific will rise
and rush into the land
and cleave all this asunder,
in a better way,
and the whales will swim
above the dunes of White Sands,
and the carcasses of old missiles
will be covered in coral,
and in the high peaks of Mescalero
people will talk about
a cloud in the shape of a mushroom
and no one will believe them,
and we will sail from Tijuana to Texas.

EL PASO, TX, 8:00 PM
BUSY HIGHWAY IN DISTANCE
QUAD AND BINAURAL MICS ON SIDE ROAD

JOEY [01.08.07]

So we can live,
instead of becoming extinct.

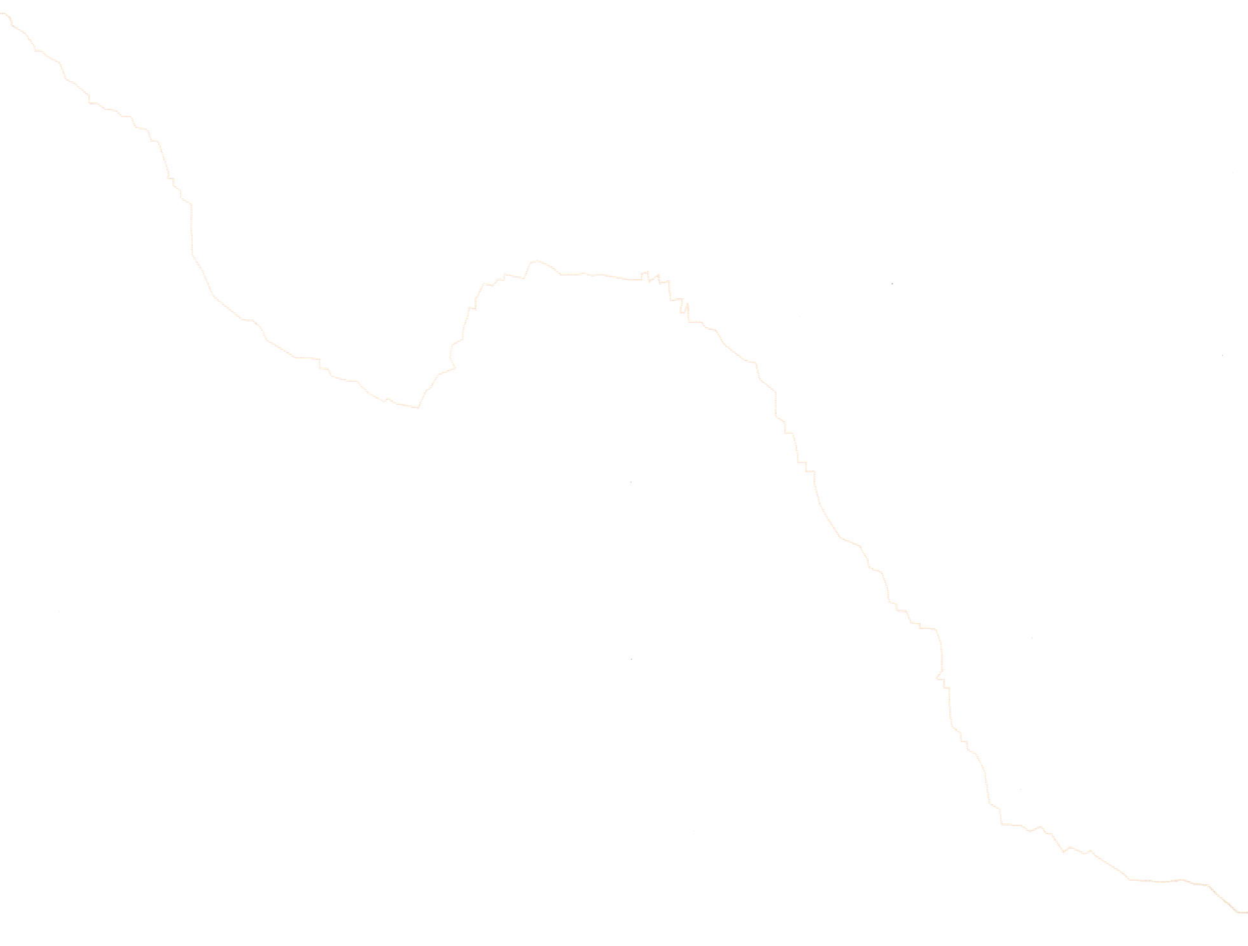

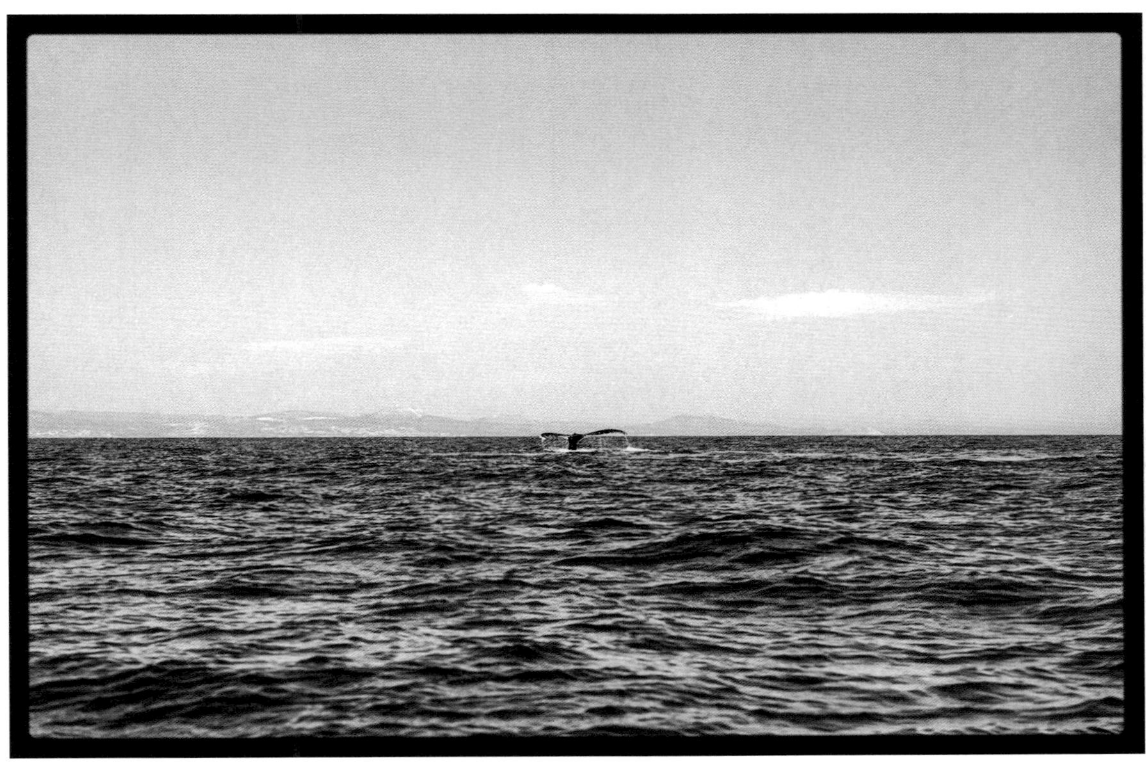

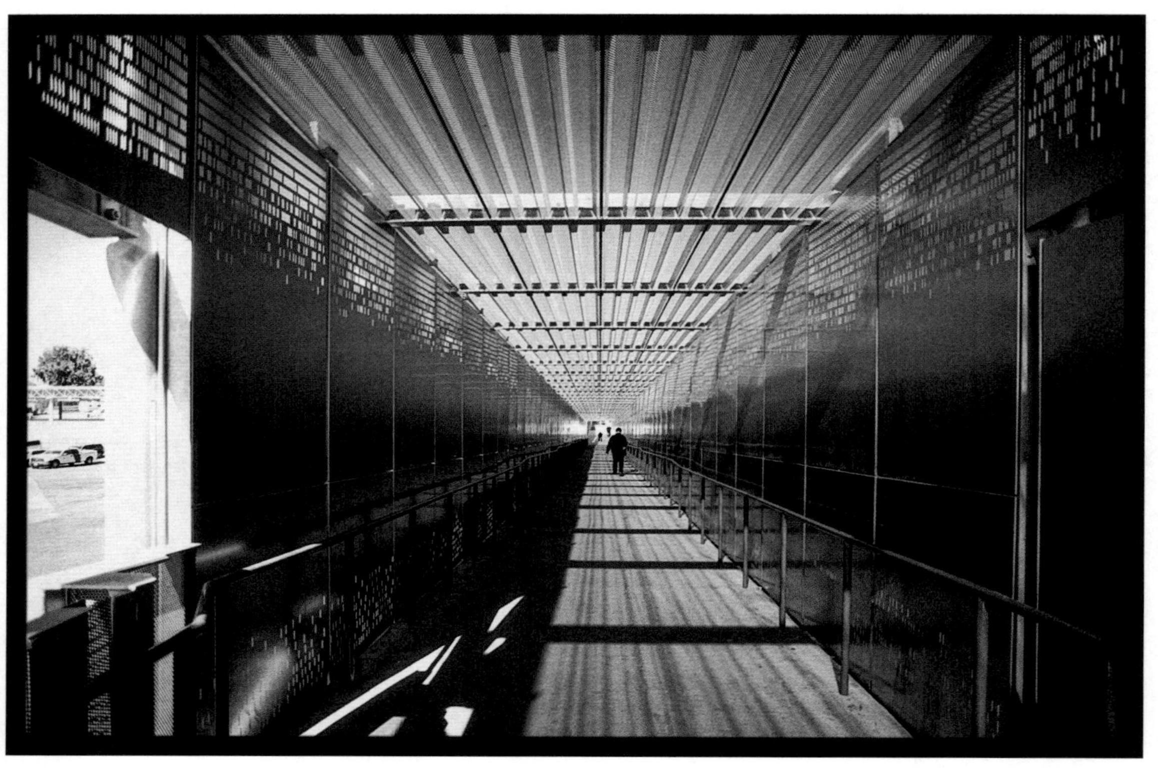

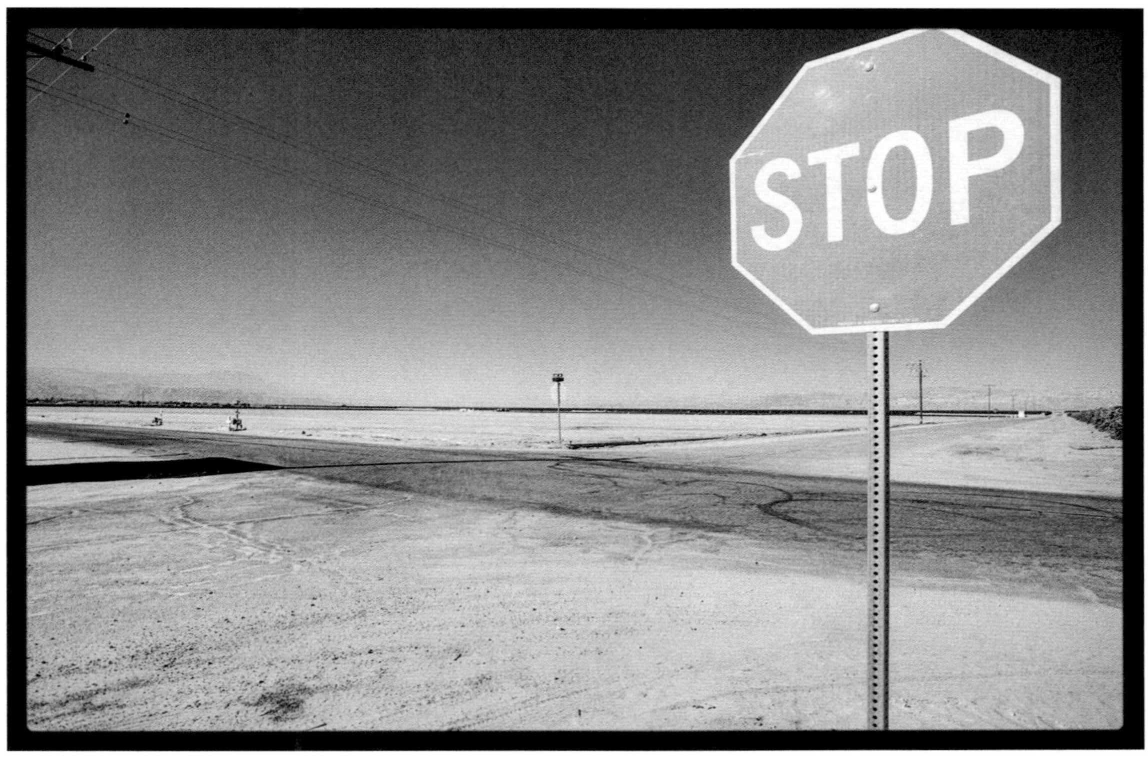
STOP

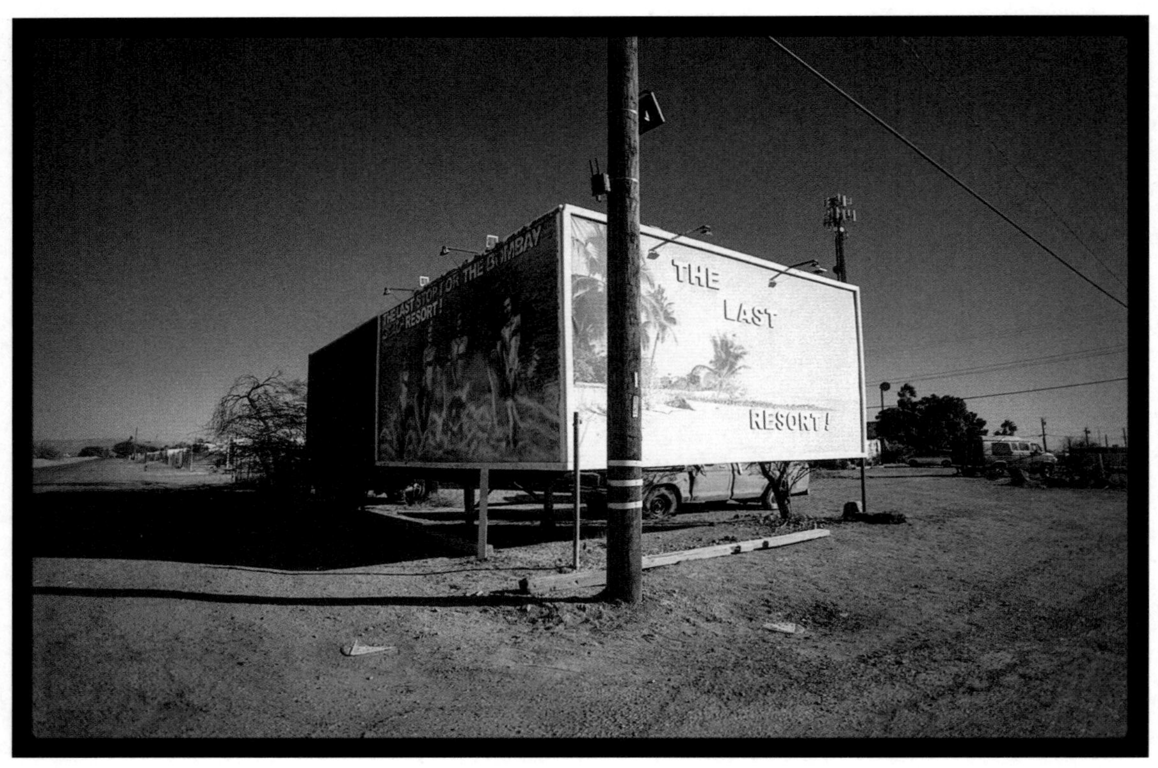
THE
LAST
RESORT!

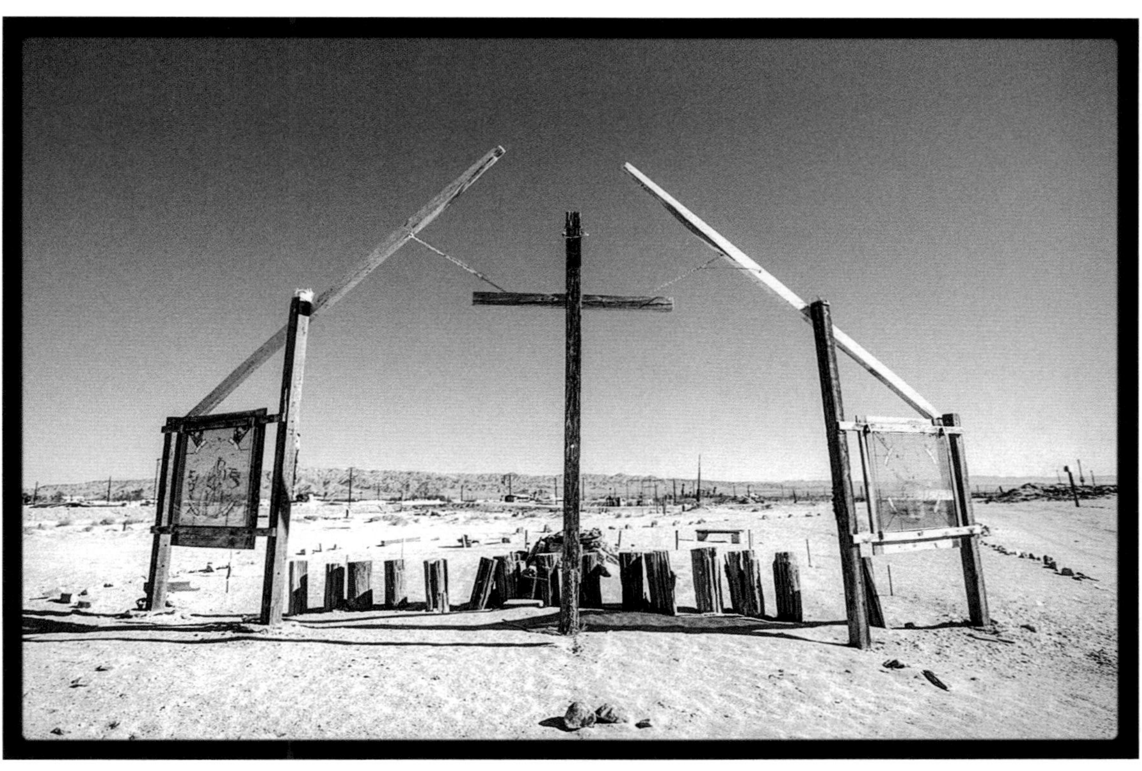

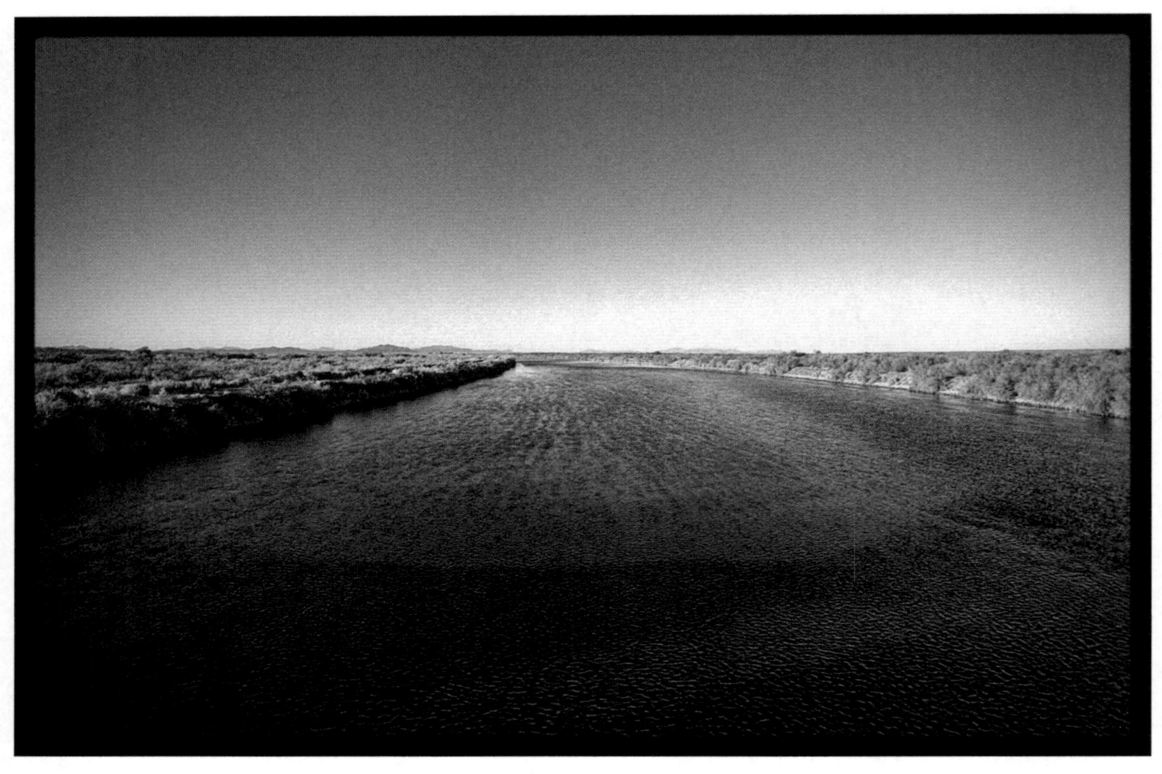

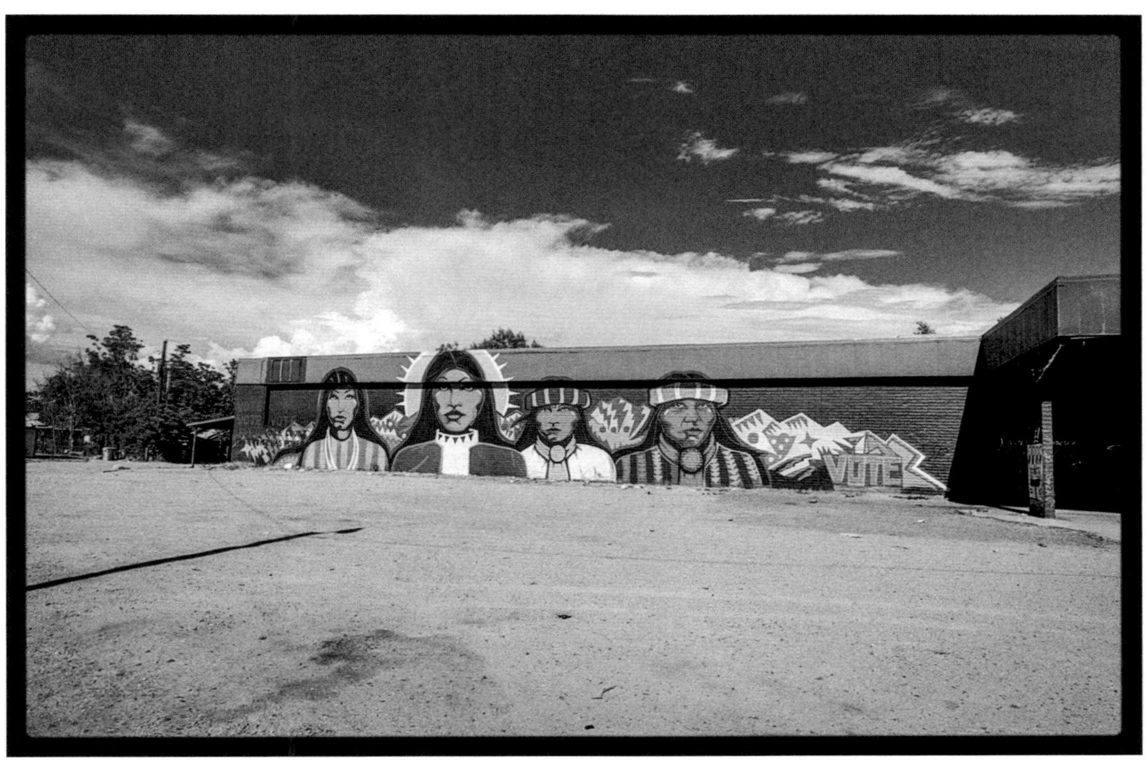
VOTE

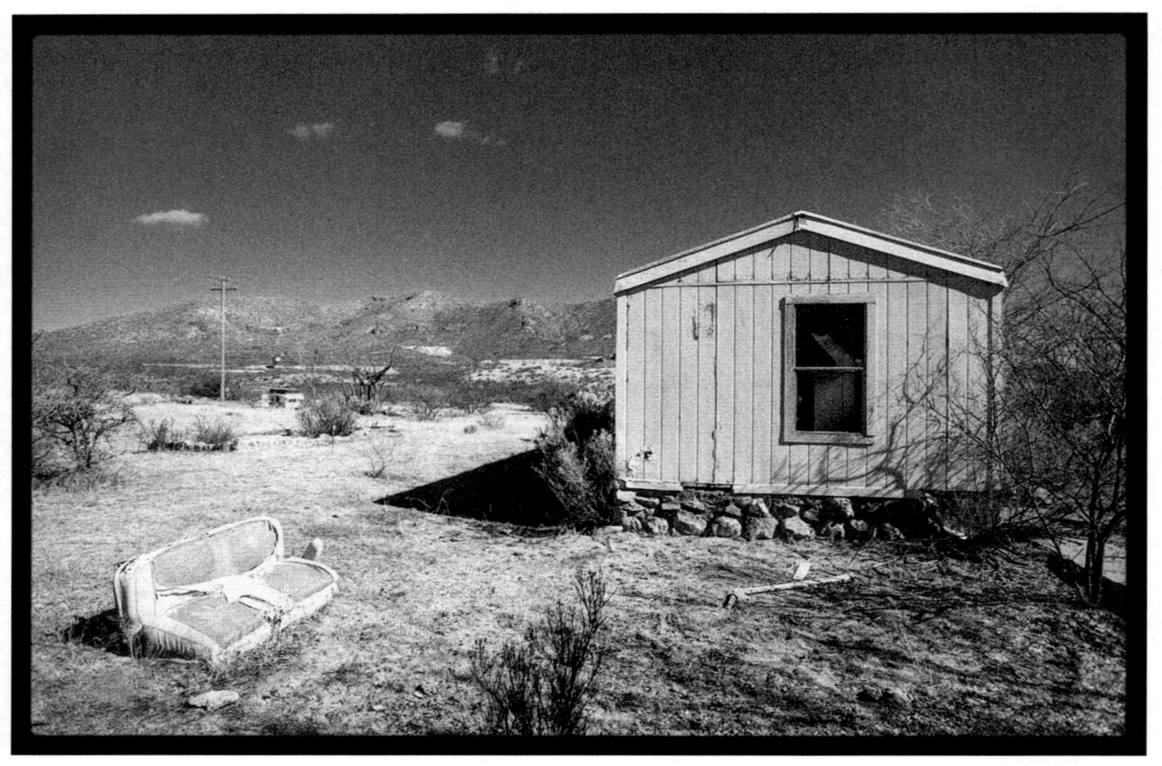

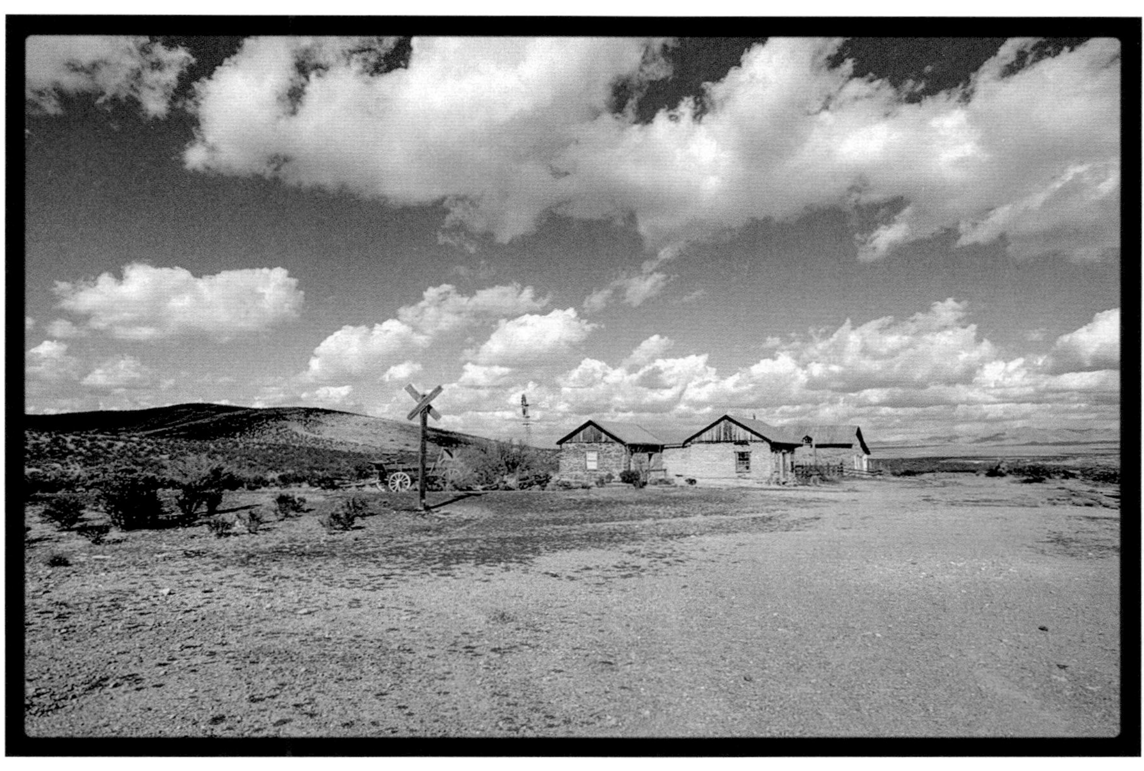

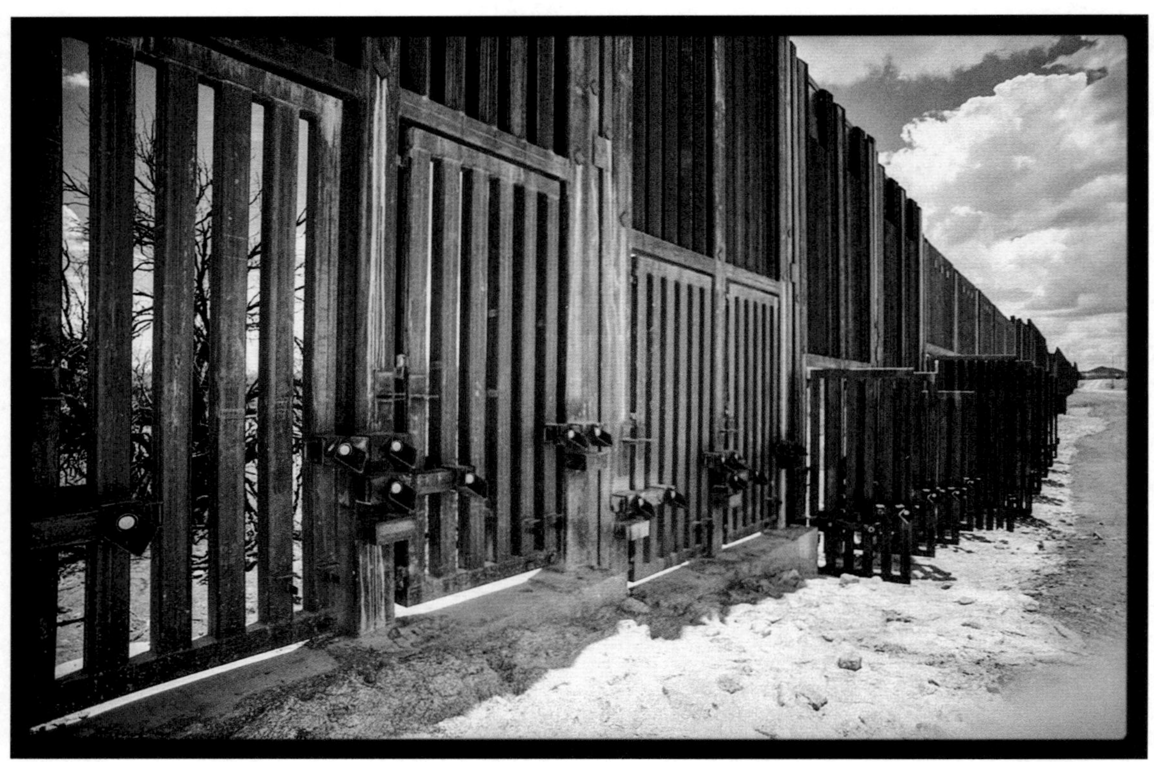

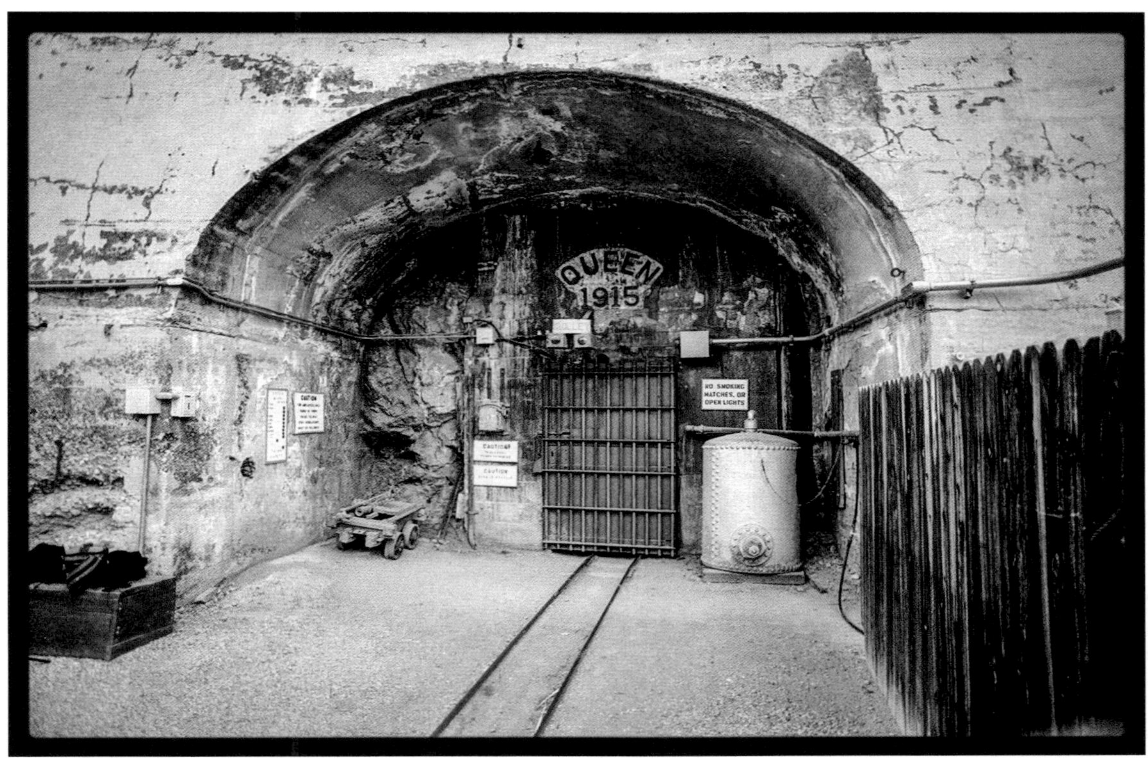
QUEEN
1915
NO SMOKING
MATCHES, OR
OPEN LIGHTS
CAUTION
CAUTION
CAUTION

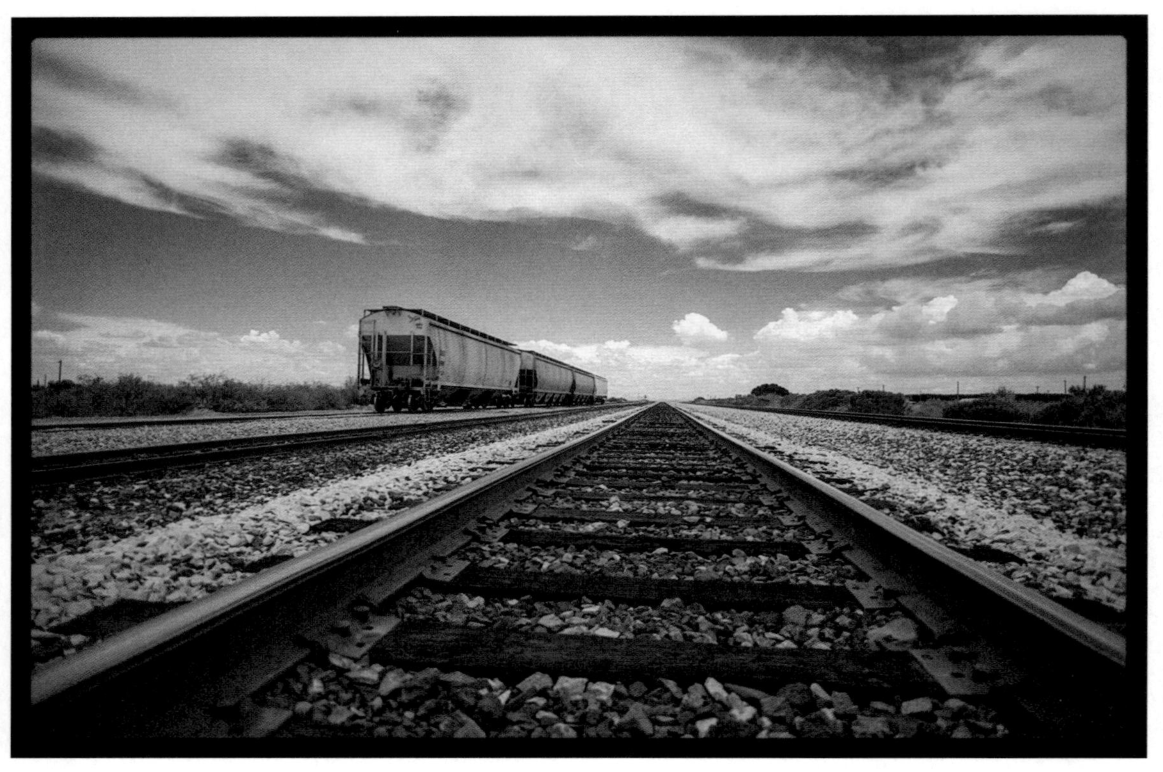

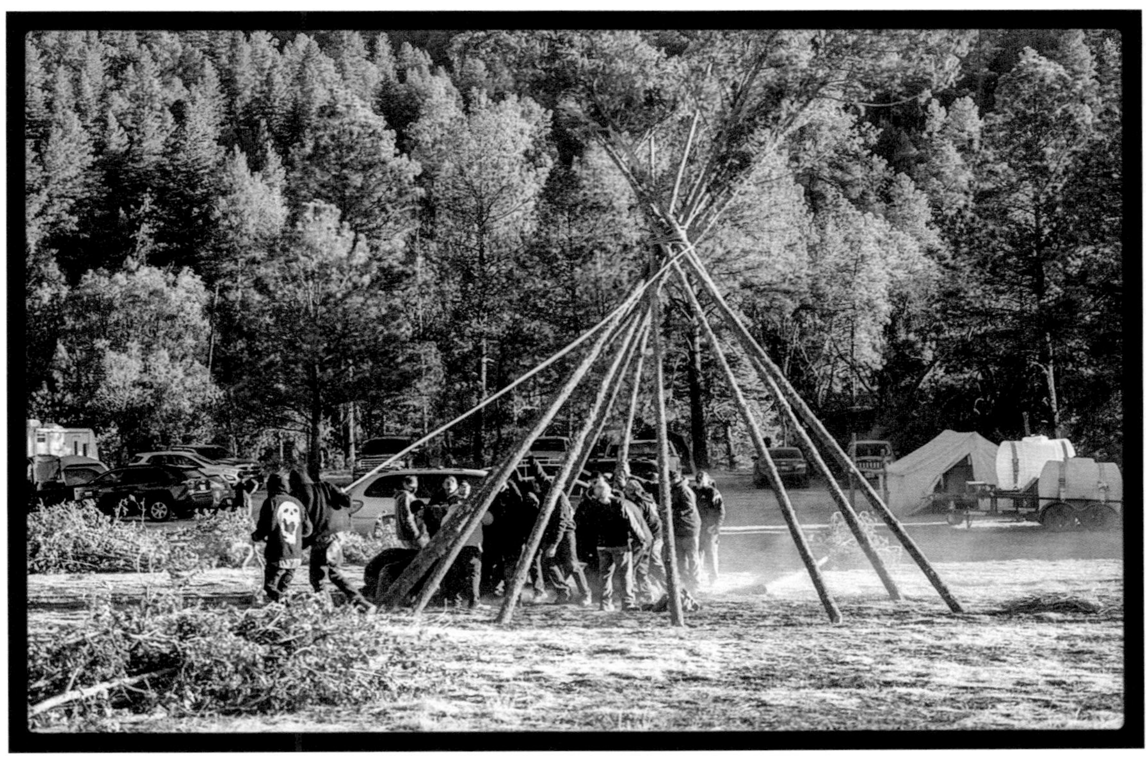

CREDITS

Voices

Maia Enrigue Luiselli
Marta López Astrain
Ella Nicolini Edwards
Ana Puente Flores
María Puente Flores
Vivir Quintana
Claudia Rodríguez Quintana

Interviewees in order of appearance

Anthony Belvado
San Carlos Reservation, Arizona

Hombre Zócalo
Mexico City

Elijah
Tohono O'odham, Arizona

Kim
Tohono O'odham, Arizona

Anthony
San Carlos Reservation, Arizona

Bertha
San Carlos Reservation, Arizona

Reenactor
Tombstone, Arizona

Doug Graeme
Copper Queen Mine, Bisbee, Arizona

Chris Dietz
Bisbee, Arizona

Arte (Ana) Romero y Carver
Santa Fe

Joey Padilla
Mescalero Reservation, New Mexico

Demetria Martinez
Santa Fe

Archival materials

Pages 22–23:
"Miracle in the Desert (Salton City Promotional Film) 1968," produced by Pro Holly Corp., 1968, posted December 12, 2021, by Our Great Salton Sea, YouTube, 12 min., 53 sec., https:/www.youtube.com/watch?v=uJrawAQon_M&t=195s.

Page 25:
Dolores Huerta, speech at the National Farm Workers Association march and rally, Sacramento, April 10, 1966, KQED, news report, 16 mm black-and-white magnetic-sound film, 6 min., 16 sec., https://diva.sfsu.edu/collections/sfbatv/bundles/185999.

Pages 26–27, 28:
Sadia Abbas, R. A. Judy, and Fred Moten, "In Conversation: Professors R. A. Judy and Fred Moten with Sadia Abbas," January 15, 2021, *Ideas & Futures*, Zoom recording, 2 hr., 16 min., 51 sec., https://ideasandfutures.com/in-conversation-professors-r-a-judy-and-fred-moten-with-sadia-abbas/.

Pages 27, 37–39:
Natalie Diaz and David Naimon, "Postcolonial Love Poem, A Conversation with Natalie Diaz," October 23, 2020, in *Between the Covers*, podcast, 2 hr., 39 min., 31 sec., https://tinhouse.com/podcast/natalie-diaz-postcolonial-love-poem/.

The artists wish to thank

Laurie Anderson, Lorena Cándano, Lucien Castaing-Taylor, Carolina Coppel, Natalie Diaz, Chris Dietz, Tammy Dietz, Bree Edwards, Steven Feld, Laura Fields, Kamilah N. Foreman, Gael García Bernal, Karen Gaytán, Alexis Lowry, Diego Luna, Humberto Moro, Fred Moten, Kat Nakaji, Fernando Peña, Karen Rasaby, Fabiola Quintero, Courtney Smith, and Elaine Trevorrow.

ABOUT THE ARTISTS

Valeria Luiselli is the author of the nonfiction books *Sidewalks* (2012) and *Tell Me How It Ends: An Essay in Forty Questions* (2017), as well as the novels *Faces in the Crowd* (2011), *The Story of My Teeth* (2013), and the internationally acclaimed *Lost Children Archive* (2019). She is the recipient of a MacArthur Fellowship (2019) and winner of a Los Angeles Times Book Prize (2014), an American Book Award (2018), Carnegie Medal (2020), Vilcek Prize for Creative Promise in Literature (2020), and a Dublin Literary Award (2021). She has been an Emerson Collective fellow, a John Simon Memorial Guggenheim fellow, and an Art for Justice Fund Bearing Witness grantee. Her work has been translated into thirty languages. Luiselli teaches at Bard College, Annandale-on-Hudson, New York, and Harvard University, Cambridge, Massachusetts. She lives in New York.

Ricardo Giraldo works in sound, contemporary classical music, and exhibition design. Having studied music in Mexico City and the Netherlands, he worked as the composer-in-residence for the Residentie Orkest of the Hague. He co-designed the permanent exhibition at the Museo Memoria y Tolerancia in Mexico City. He directed the documentary film festival Ambulante (2009–10), as well as Cinema23 and the Fénix Film Awards (2012–19). Together with Gael García Bernal and Diego Luna, he founded the podcast division of the production company La Corriente del Golfo. He co-created the podcasts *La advertencia* (The Warning, 2020), *Mujeres de fuego* (Women of Fire, 2021), and *Las guardianas* (The Guardians, 2023), and the audiobook *Desierto Sonoro* (Lost Children Archive, 2020) by Valeria Luiselli, among other projects. He lives in Mexico City.

Leo Heiblum is a composer, producer, and sound artist. He studied piano and composition in Mexico City, tabla in India, son jarocho in Veracruz, and Latin American music in Argentina. He has collaborated with Philip Glass on albums such as *Concert of the Sixth Sun* (2013), *Introducing the Suso/Glass Quartet* (2018), and *The Spirit of the Earth* (2018). Most recently, he collaborated with Patti Smith and Soundwalk Collective on *The Perfect Vision* album trilogy (2019–22) and the exhibition *Evidence* at the Centre Pompidou, Paris (2022–23). He has scored over forty feature films, many of which received awards at major international film festivals. He has won four Ariel (2009, 2013, 2014, and 2024) and two Fénix awards (2016 and 2018). His album *Encyclopedia Sonica Vol.1* was released in 2024. He lives in Tepoztlán, Mexico.

This book was published in conjunction with the exhibition *Echoes from the Borderlands* at Dia Chelsea, New York, December 11, 2024–March 1, 2025.

All exhibitions at Dia are made possible by the Economou Exhibition Fund.

Echoes from the Borderlands is curated by Kamilah N. Foreman, director of publications, and Humberto Moro, deputy director of program.

Echoes from the Borderlands is organized in partnership with the Institute for Studies on Latin American Art (ISLAA).

Echoes from the Borderlands was developed at Dia Art Foundation; the ArtLab at Harvard University, Cambridge, Massachusetts; BeluRecords, Mexico City; and La Corriente del Golfo Podcast, Mexico City; with the generous support of Laurie Gunst and Karen Yamashita.

First printing, 2024

Dia Art Foundation
535 West 22nd Street
New York, New York 10011
diaart.org

Distributed by
Artbook | DAP
75 Broad Street, Suite 630
New York, New York 10004
artbook.com

Designer: Laura Fields
Editor: Karen Rasaby
Rights and reproduction: Jenn Kane
Proofreaders: Nicolás Guerrero and Svetlana Kitto

Typeset in Courier and Helvetica Neue
Printed on Munken 100 gsm and Colorplan 175 gsm
Printed and bound in Spain by Brizzolis, S. A., Madrid

ISBN: 978-0-944521-62-5

Library of Congress Control Number: 2024948155